Bold Visions
for the *Garden*

Bold Visions
for the *Garden*

Richard Hartlage

Fulcrum Publishing
Golden, Colorado

For Silas Mountsier and Graeme Hardie,
in grateful appreciation for a decade of patronage,
collaboration, and friendship.

Library of Congress Cataloging-in-Publication Data

Hartlage, Richard W.
Bold visions for the garden : basics, magic & inspiration /
Richard W. Hartlage.
    p. cm.
Includes bibliographical references (p.   ).
  ISBN 1-55591-316-4 (pbk.)
 1. Landscape gardening. I. Title.
  SB473 .H387 2001

                    712'.6–dc21
                    2001003268

Printed and bound in China
0 9 8 7 6 5 4 3 2 1

Editing and Design by Watershed Books
Front cover photograph by Richard Hartlage

Fulcrum Publishing
16100 Table Mountain Parkway, Suite 300
Golden, Colorado 80403
(800) 992-2908 • (303) 277-1623
www.fulcrum-books.com

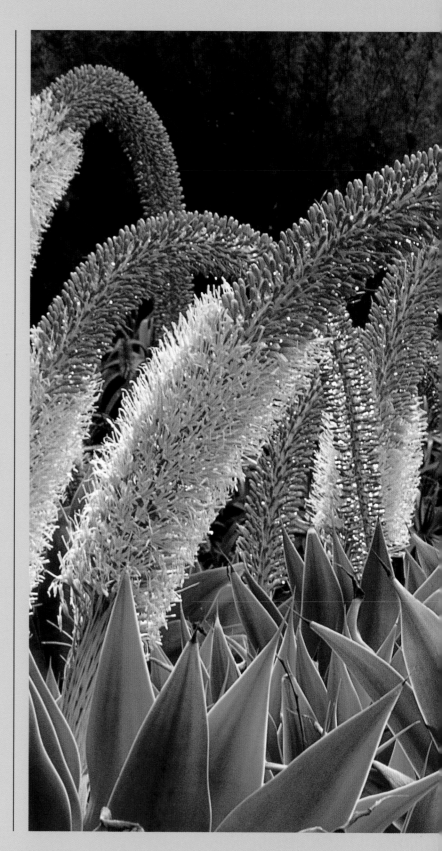

FRONT COVER: *Tulip 'Marjolein' with a background of*
Cordyline australis *'Albertii'*. **FRONTISPIECE:** *This lovely*
planting of spring ephemerals in blue and white is **Corydalis**
flexuosa *'Blue Panda',* **Anemone nemerosa** *'Vestal',* **Muscari**
armeniacum, *and the pale blue one is 'Valerie Finnis'*. **TITLE**
PAGE: *Ann and Sam Davis's garden in El Paso, Texas, designed*
by Martha Schwartz. **ACKNOWLEDGMENTS:** *Arching flower*
spikes of **Agave attenuata**.

Acknowledgments

Gardening is a vast world of passionate people, each dedicated to realizing his or her vision of paradise. I am grateful to the garden owners, makers, and designers for their generosity, knowledge, and our common passion. Thank you to all those who have opened their world to me so I could capture their work on film and, more important, learn more about the craft and art of making gardens. Thank you to my clients—you know who you are—for trusting me with your gardens and allowing me to publish them here.

I will be forever grateful to Constance Bollen, who designed this book and, more to the point, who bought into this harebrained idea and pitched it to her business partners: Andrea Jarvela, who has guided this text with an unerring hand, and Nancy Duncan-Cashman, who has made sure the highest production standards possible were realized. These, the women of Watershed Books, are most responsible for making this book reality. Bringing *Bold Visions* to print with you has been nothing but a delight in spite of the deadlines—thanks for believing in me and for all the laughs along the way. To Marlene Blessing at Fulcrum Publishing, whose zany humor and zest for life are infectious, and whose vision and guidance have made this book better at every turn.

To Jerry Harpur, who has taught me to take better pictures; I stand in awe of your ability, and your encouragement in making gardens has been invaluable.

Thanks could never be complete without acknowledging the great group of people I work with on a daily basis at the Elisabeth C. Miller Botanical Garden—to Greg Graves, who makes sure the garden is always looking its best; to Richie Steffen, who watches over our most prized plants with precision and infinite concern; to Linda Evangelista, who makes sure we are paid on time, among other things; to Linda Plato, who makes dreams come true; to Christey Bahn, who helps to educate gardeners in the Pacific Northwest; to Rebecca Stewart, Colleen Weinstein, and Beverly Bodine, who spent 2000 weeding; to Frank Minton, for smoothing the rough spots; and to my board of directors, who support my efforts on their behalf. I think Betty would be proud.

Last and by no means least, thanks to Tim Teuten, who has listened to the woes of writing this book, shared in my excitement at seeing it materialize, and provided nothing but encouragement and support in spite of the mood swings.

Foreword

BY VALERIE EASTON

From the moment Richard Hartlage walked into my office one afternoon in November 1995 to ask my thoughts on his accepting the job as director of the Elisabeth C. Miller Botanical Garden, we've been fast friends. Over the years we've talked gardens more days than not, and he has generously shared his expertise, made me laugh, and forced me to clarify my own ideas about plants and gardens. Most of all, he has pushed me to see gardens in new and surprising ways. In his first book, Richard brings the force of his vision and personality to bear in both photos and words, so you too will feel the pleasure of being challenged to look at garden-making with a fresh eye. Richard exudes energy, wit, and originality, as well as an unparalleled fervor for plants and gardens. He abundantly shares these attributes in *Bold Visions for the Garden.*

As a horticultural librarian at the University of Washington for the past sixteen years, I've purchased and used thousands of gardening books. Yet I'm struck with the freshness of *Bold Visions,* as it is an unabashed celebration of the visual. And after all, don't most of us indulge in ornamental gardening for the sheer, changeable, magical beauty of it? The soft, washy pink of a tree peony, the thickly ribbed pleating of a leaf, or the magnificence of a backlit drift of tulips draws us in so that we're endlessly beguiled and irrevocably enchanted by this dirty, expensive, and time-eating obsession.

Richard has written a very personal book (you'll learn that his bathroom is painted turquoise, his dining room sunshine yellow), and the story of his odyssey toward an understanding of garden design and the people who have helped him along the way is fascinating. It is not only the gardens pictured in the book that are rich and multilayered, but also Richard's evolution as a garden designer, including his errors: "One year we planted soft lavender tulips (thousands of them). We never repeated that mistake." And don't think that because Richard is visionary in his approach it means he isn't practical. Useful advice punctuates his enthusiasms, as in "I think of a garden as being built in layers." The first layer is the ideas, then come the primary (walls, walkways) and the secondary (small trees and shrubs) structures, and third is the "fluff" (containers, art, perennials, etc.). Plant lover that he is, Richard emphasizes again and again, in both text and photos, that boldness lies not just in plant choice, but in the clarity of the garden's plan, the unity of its design concept.

The diversity of the gardens pictured is dazzling, both stylistically and geographically. As you look at public and private gardens, ranging from San Francisco landscape architect Topher Delaney's hospital garden for kids in San Diego, California, to a small private garden overlooking English Bay in Vancouver, British Columbia, it is clear that all too often garden books reflect a single aesthetic. Not this one. And why shouldn't we consider everything from adobe walls to formal hedging, from echeveria to lamb's ears, for it pays to remember that we have this entire, exciting range of materials and styles available to us as the raw stuff of garden-making. Perhaps Richard makes his points most effectively with dramatic photos, as in the square walled room in a Texas garden, empty save for a starkly vertical cactus and a tiny square window, all as austere as a monk's cell. Here is an author as comfortable discussing agaves as he is considering roses and poppies. Pink walls studded with nails are as lovingly photographed as European hornbeams elegantly pruned into the shape of Gothic windows. The chapter on form and texture advocates not only spiky or large-leafed plants, but also a garden pyramid made of hundreds of bowling balls, and inverted terra-cotta triangles that serve as hanging baskets. The book is eye-opening.

By the time you finish *Bold Visions*, you'll have a clear and compelling picture of the colors, shapes, plants, and gardens that Richard loves. There are far less effective ways to learn about stunning gardens. ∎

Valerie Easton writes the weekly column "Plant Life" for the Seattle Times' Pacific Northwest *magazine, is published in a wide variety of gardening magazines, and is coauthor of* Artists in Their Gardens *(Sasquatch Books, 2001).*

Defining Your Vision

To my way of seeing, a garden is not

a succession of small rooms or little effects

but one large tableau, whose elements

are inextricably linked to the

accomplishment of the entire garden,

just as in a painting all passages

conduce to the effect of the whole.

~

Robert Dash,

Notes from Madoo

A striking combination of crimson-striped Phormium
'Color Guard' with the fleeting scarlet blooms of Geum
'Red Wings' creates enough tension between the shades of
red to be eye-catching but not jarring.

Why do you garden? This is an essential question to ask. Is it to make a place to hold your plant collection? To extend your living space into the out-of-doors? Because you have an insatiable need to see things grow? Because you have a creative spirit that cannot be stopped, and a garden is yet another canvas? Because it

▲ *In this Texas garden, colored adobe creates a Mondrian-like effect. The strong colors hold their own in the hot sun of an El Paso summer, and the ten-inch nails introduce a pattern that is simultaneously beautiful and repulsive. The portals through the series of rooms lure you to explore this incredible garden further.*

▼ *A traditional cottage planting style is anything but ordinary, with chartreuse sweet potato vine, elephant ears, Persian shield, and other tender and hardy perennials against the blue walls. The diagonal angles of the walls dramatically emphasize the change in grade, and the cobalt against the midnight blue exaggerates the illusion of depth in this small space.*

is good physical exercise? Maybe to keep up with the neighbors?

I started gardening because I love plants. Now I garden because I thrive on the creative possibilities. Gardening is so endless in its opportunities, one could argue that it is only the brave or foolhardy who consider trying to make

a garden. The fortunes that will be spent. The hours of planning, worrying, and redesigning. Then there is the maintenance—endless weeding, planting, replanting, sweeping, and cleaning—all to keep your garden in tiptop condition.

Is it all worth it? Yes. It is worth it. Little else in life encompasses such vast knowledge—from the science of growing plants to the design and art training that enables us to organize plants and other elements to make a place called a garden. For me, a garden starts with an idea, an organizing theme. Tradition weighs heavily here. You can make a garden that reflects the aesthetic of Gertrude Jekyll, the early-twentieth-century English garden designer and author of *Color Schemes for the Flower Garden*, with lush naturalistic sweeps of plants from the four corners of the world. Or you could look to the Italians for inspiration to create a more classical architecture, with clipped trees and shrubs as living extensions of a classical home. You may be inspired by Ludwig Mies van der Rohe and follow the "less is more" principle. Or perhaps you'll look to the most current designers, who embrace a little of each of these

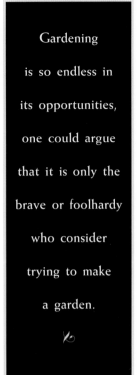

Gardening is so endless in its opportunities, one could argue that it is only the brave or foolhardy who consider trying to make a garden.

schemes while injecting a sense of humor and drama. Two ladies on opposite coasts—landscape architect Martha Schwartz in Boston and landscape designer Topher Delaney in San Francisco—do just that. Or maybe you will want a garden inspired by nature, such as the meadow gardens of Piet Oudolf, famed Dutch nurseryman and garden designer.

I love landscape architecture, and I love horticulture. The two disciplines need not be mutually exclusive: they marry beautifully. It is this marriage that most inspires me—when thoughtful garden architecture and deft horti-culture converge to create a unique place. There is a garden style to suit any person, site, situation, and taste. When I first meet clients, I like to visit them in their home, on their turf, so I can consciously take in countless details. I note the architectural style of the house and whether the décor complements it. I find out if they have children or pets and see whether the house is immaculately clean or is more "lived in." I ask how much gardening they currently do themselves. This information is essential to making a garden that will suit them. Inconsistencies in any of the aforementioned factors are red flags that require further discussion. Next, I ask more inter-active questions. Do they entertain? What style gardens do they like? Do they have a particular vision in mind? Will they maintain their new garden, or hire someone? What physical needs do they wish to have met in the new spaces?

◄ The beautifully sculptural agave looks like the head of Medusa against the curving wall. The warm terra-cotta orange is a perfect color under the Arizona sun in April. Desert ephemerals provide dots of sunshine yellow and coral to make a striking scene that utilizes both sumptuous color and striking form.

▶ *The jade blue of this aloe,* **Aloe plicatilis,** *is refreshing in the arid Southern California climate. The color is soothing and cool. Blue foliage always adds a subtle sense of relief to the green background of any garden. Blue-leafed hostas can provide the same effect in a shady temperate garden. If you have sun, plant blue fescues. Short-lived, they are lovely nonetheless.*

How much money do they want to spend? Legions of people who make gardens never ask themselves these questions, but the best gardens start with the answers. It takes a clear and single-minded vision about where you are headed in your garden to accomplish your goals.

While planning and vision do not preclude the role serendipity will play, both function and style are essential to making a garden that is aesthetically satisfying while providing places for children, pets, and friends, and—as the case may be—hiding the garbage cans, screening the hot tub, or accommodating the barbecue grill. Clear and obvious circulation patterns are important: how you get to the front door, and whether that route is different than the way your guests will approach. Which site features are assets or liabilities that need to be overcome. All these considerations may make building a garden seem daunting to the timid of heart, but when each is considered in turn—not simultaneously—the solutions will be apparent and the process can take shape.

Once practical matters have been addressed, the fun starts. I love sitting down with a piece of paper and figuring out how the spaces of a new garden will work:

how they will link to the house and to each other; what construction materials will be used, and how; what trees will be planted and where. A vision begins to materialize. I think about special plant arrangements and move on to paths, walls, and ceilings—the basic elements of design. A cedar fence along the periphery of the back garden, brick walks, and a spare modern style that is asymmetrically arranged may complement a new addition to the house. If the client wants a jungle, I can use golden honey locusts and giant reed grass and red buckeyes and divide the garden into two major planting areas, even if it is as modest as fifty feet square. The area nearest the house can be planted with large-scale perennials and dramatic shrubs, such as the variegated devil's walking stick, to surround and impress the visitor in the way a jungle would. The lower area can be planted with a mix of low plants to provide a sense of open space and relief from the upper garden.

The garden I've just described is that of my friend and client Graeme Hardie, who lives in Nutley, New Jersey (page 13). I wanted to make a place where Graeme could entertain, and that would provide endless journeys. The garden's geometry reflects the quirky lines of the house, and it is rich in plants and whimsical elements. I think of a garden as being built in layers. The first layer is the ideas; then come the primary structures, such as walls, walks, and large trees; followed by the secondary structures, such as small trees and shrubs. Finally, there is the "fluff"—the fun details and accents, such as containers, sculpture, furniture, perennials, bulbs, and annuals. This is a vast generalization, but it is the formula most design professionals use to make a garden. This doesn't mean that a garden cannot be fashioned over years—it doesn't have to be thought out in total before you first shove spade into soil. But logic is an essential tool: each new element, space, or plant that you add should relate to those that already exist. Follow the thread in as clear a manner as possible. If you do, you will end up with a garden that responds to the architecture of your home, one that meets your functional needs, and—most important—one that is beautiful and inspiring. A garden of delight, with a bold and clear vision that is yours. ■

Setting

The perfect site is on a slightly rising ground
with large healthy trees, a fine view, or a
beautiful background of foliage; it has deep rich
topsoil and is oriented to be out of the wind—but
catch the sunshine. As long as we are dreaming,
we might as well add that it be near schools,
churches, and shops and that utilities are
already at the property line.
If you find it, buy it.

~

THOMAS CHURCH,

Gardens Are for People

Tom Hobbs's and Brent Beattie's back terrace commands
breathtaking views of English Bay and the skyscrapers
of Vancouver, British Columbia, which are perfectly framed
by windmill palm, Trachycarpus fortunei. The chaise lounge
invites you to while away the afternoon admiring the view.

Setting is an obvious and primary criterion to take into account when building a garden. There are two kinds of gardens: those that look out onto the world, and those that focus in on themselves. There are more of the latter than the former. Not all of us are blessed with spectacular views. Most of us have a need for privacy, thus we seek ways to screen ourselves from our neighbors. A feeling of refuge is also an innate desire, and many people go to great lengths to achieve it in their gardens. Fences, hedges, and large-scale plantings that create borders are very often the first things to be installed in a new garden. We want our space to be our own private world.

If you happen to be blessed with a spectacular view, don't deny it. I know of a single-minded plant collector in Seattle, Washington, who couldn't resist the urge to add one more tree to his property. Eventually he planted away his splendid view of Puget Sound and the Olympic Mountains. Everyone who visits this man's garden wants to see the view,

but he is insulted that they do not want to see his plants. Why would you want to deny such commanding natural features when you can have it all—your view and your vegetation, too.

I have lived in the southeastern and northeastern United States, and now I live in the Pacific Northwest. Each of these regions is temperate, and each has its own distinctive personality, formed by climate, soils, vegetation, geology, and topography. These physical characteristics tell us much about our location in the world and create a strong sense of place, and are thus comforting. I love the Pacific Northwest and can hardly imagine living anywhere else. The quality of light here is magical. I don't even begrudge the cloudy days: the moody atmospheric skies make me appreciate the clear days all the more. My favorite light is under a high overcast sky with just a few cloud breaks, so when you hold your arm out there is just the hint of a fuzzy shadow. Pale colors look best in diffuse light, which we get a lot of here in spring, early summer, and fall. Driving south on Interstate 5 on my way home from work, the sight of

▲ *Wave Hill in the Bronx, New York, is one of my favorite public gardens. Reminiscent of late-nineteenth-century estates, it commands spectacular views of the Hudson River and the New Jersey Palisades. This arbor, laden with glories from the summer garden, creates an intimate place from which to see the grand view.*

▶ *The flower garden at Wave Hill, lovely as it is, offers an opportunity to soak up the incredible setting.* **Nicotiana sylvestris** *and* **Verbena bonariensis** *provide flower color late in the summer.*

▲ *The formality of the yews in Italian containers provides a strong focus in Wave Hill's flower garden, but the Palisades are ever present in the distance.*

◀ *The Wave Hill flower garden seems all the more domestic in scale compared to the heroic rock walls and the great Hudson River.*

Mount Rainier, a sleeping volcano looming over the city, never fails to awe me. The gray waters of Puget Sound, Lake Washington, and Lake Union—as moody as the sky they reflect—are also part of my daily existence.

The Elisabeth C. Miller Botanical Garden, where I work, sits on a high bluff looking across Puget Sound to

Bainbridge Island, and beyond it the Olympic Mountains. It is a spectacular setting for a garden. There are just enough Douglas firs to frame the view and create a sense of majesty. I dislike sites with all the vegetation stripped away—denuded like a crude landing strip. Grand views, such as the one from Miller Garden, draw us into the environment. They should be integrated into the garden, not separated from it by a vast, empty foreground. If space allows, use larger-scale trees to frame an expansive view. If your garden is small, use plants that are appropriately scaled to the garden space and the view beyond.

I grew up outside Louisville, Kentucky, so another setting that is burned into my psyche is rolling hills with deciduous hardwood forests and an agrarian landscape. I have worked with this kind

There are two kinds of gardens: those that look out onto the world, and those that focus in on themselves.

▲ *The soft yellow wall at the entrance to this property in Scottsdale, Arizona, complements the red-brown of the mountains in the distance. The wall and the palo verde trees provide a lovely foreground, but they also serve a practical purpose: screening the unsightly road from view.*

◀ *In Seattle, Washington, Mount Rainier looms large over the city and never goes unappreciated on clear days. Such a view is prized, and it leaves no doubt you are in the Pacific Northwest.*

of scenery twice as a professional. The first time was in North Carolina, at Chatwood, the former garden of Mrs. Helen Watkins. Her house and garden were nestled in fields and woods. My favorite view on the property is upon leaving the formal rose garden, looking downhill through a grass meadow framed with red cedars and roses climbing on pillars (pages 28–29). The path organizes the scene and makes for a picturesque, romantic setting. Many people dismiss the simple beauty of a pasture, yet a meadow is a wonder to watch through the seasons. The meadow grasses are a fresh yellow-green in the spring when they first emerge, then flower in early summer, turn golden tan as the seeds ripen, and finally age to brown. Mowing this type of meadow once a year in late fall or early winter allows the flowering perennials to seed and establish themselves. If you mow in the summer, the plants never reach flower size and complete their life cycle. You also need to keep trees out so that the meadow stays open and is not overtaken by natural succession. I love a meadow laced with oxeye daisies, goldenrod, butterfly weed, iron weed, and countless other meadow flowers.

A pastoral scene on a larger scale, Willowwood Arboretum in Chester, New Jersey (pages 30–31), has acres of rolling fields beautifully framed by groves of conifers and deciduous hardwoods. Tens of thousands of daffodils were planted in one meadow, creating great ribbons of gold. My favorite time of year at Willowwood is autumn. The meadows are covered in the native little bluestem grass, which turns russet in October against a backdrop of gold, orange, and scarlet tulip poplars, maples, and oaks. It is spectacular.

Wooded settings can be lovely and enchanting, but they do need to be managed. Trees in a forest can grow too close, leaving too little light and too little room for

---

▶ *Plantings and setting merge seamlessly in this garden, with its staggering collection of old climbing roses. Early-twentieth-century varieties and species too large for formal gardens are trained up eight-foot-tall poles, creating a romantic statement in this pastoral landscape. The path draws the eye in and beckons you on.*

the observer to appreciate their aesthetic effect. If it is a forest setting you desire, be brave. Thin the trees, keeping only the most beautiful ones, thus allowing more light to reach the ground. This is hard for many people to do because they consider trees sacrosanct. But gardens need

▲ *Willowwood Arboretum in Chester, New Jersey, contains seemingly miles of walks through the arboretum and the meadows on the 150-acre property. My favorite strolls are through the fields in the autumn. This particular walk wends through groves of red spruce and collections of winter hazels, which flower in early March, and leads you to the edge of this field of little bluestem, a grass native to New Jersey. As you cross the meadow, mature conifers frame the view back to the nineteenth-century clapboard farmhouse.*

▶ *On an even larger scale at Willowwood, the meadows are vast and beautiful in late September. They celebrate the agricultural heritage of the area and provide relief from the densely planted collections of trees elsewhere on the property. You can smell the autumn air and feel the waning sun on your face.*

good editing to bring out their strongest attributes. This is a hard lesson to learn, accept, and practice, but balancing the light and root competition is essential if you wish to have a successful woodland garden.

Natural wonders make for lovely views, but so do man-made ones. Gardeners lucky enough to have an urban view can see the spectacle of city life by day and the magic of skyscrapers alight against a darkened sky at night. One of the most spectacular roof gardens I've ever visited is atop Rockefeller Center. I don't know who designed these highly formal parterres, but they form a perfect oasis juxtaposed against the looming architecture of Fifth Avenue. One especially disarming vantage point faces the intricate façade of St. Patrick's Cathedral across the street.

A distant cityscape is a different type of urban view. The garden of my friends Thomas Hobbs and Brent Beattie looks across English Bay to the city of Vancouver, British Columbia (pages 20–21). They have the best of both worlds—a city view in a quiet nonurban setting.

Even if you don't have a spectacular view, you can create your own. Mirrors are a great illusion to expand the garden and fool the eye. Place one at the end of a path

---

◀ *Modern design principles are a striking element in this enchanted woodland. The forest has been thinned so that each tree can be seen and appreciated. The circular pools and the moss-covered pyramid in the center of the largest one make this garden of greens seem mystical. The sound of water and the cool shade lull you into another reality.*

If you do not have the luxury of a view of great natural wonders, create one with windows into your own garden. They create a larger sense of space and mystery in small gardens. Get the most impact by arranging these glimpses from one garden room to another along primary axes.

and frame it like a window. Your guests will be startled to suddenly see someone headed in their direction. This trick works best when the mirror can be attached to a fence or structure and framed like a window to enhance the ploy. Windows that open from one area of the garden into another are also great fun (opposite page). Cut a hole in a fence separating two garden rooms to create a larger sense of space. This is very effective if the views or center lines are arranged to line up.

Beyond views of natural wonders, you can use familiar plants in the garden proper to make the most of your own region. By integrating local native plants with commonly grown exotics, you acknowledge the regional quality of native flora. This is crucially important in arid climates—why irrigate to excess in the Southwest, for example, when there are so many sculptural desert plants at the gardener's disposal? I dream of doing a desert garden—the plants are so dramatic they seem otherworldly, and the setting is so beautiful and austere. Master garden maker Steve Martino of Scottsdale, Arizona, creates gardens that celebrate the native Southwest landscape with the plants he uses and with the colors he paints his stucco architecture (page 27).

Acknowledging the setting of your garden is essential to integrating it with its natural surroundings, whether mountain, water, urban, or pastoral views. The plants you choose, the stones for paths, even the colors you pick for your garden walls should all meld. ∎

Architecture

While built elements are a powerful way

to achieve unity in the garden's layout,

it is important to execute them

with a light touch. Sculpting the earth,

selecting materials, lining up details

and meeting corners, treating edges,

creating water features —

all contrive to carry out the genius of place.

~

WOLFGANG OEHME, JAMES VAN SWEDEN,

SUSAN RADEMACHER,

Bold Romantic Gardens

Topher Delaney is one of the most daring of today's garden designers. Her work is sculptural in quality and always innovative. These dynamic curved walls in the Leichtag Family Healing Garden at Children's Hospital in San Diego, California, transcend the functional needs of boundary; they are visually engaging and boisterous.

◀ *The layers of walls draw you through the garden into the heart of the place. Ceramic birds and animal cutouts offer whimsical relief on the surfaces of this wall.*

The best gardens use their allotted space well. By that I mean gardens should respond to the architecture of the house or building they are tied to, make some nod to the region they are built in, be logical in the way you move through them, and be a strong expression of the owner's taste. Gardens are places, and a place needs walls, floors, and ceilings to define it. These basic components can be manipulated in millions of ways, with an infinite number of materials and variations. That is where the excitement lies.

If you are a traditionalist, you may draw your inspiration from historical models. My first job in horticulture was on the private estate of Mrs. Helen Watkins in Hillsborough, North Carolina. Mrs. Watkins collects old roses; her garden is sweet and, in the second and third weeks of May, when the roses flower, it is intoxicating. The colors are subtle and languid: somber wines, the palest pinks, creams and whites, pale yellow, and dusky mauve, with a few strongly colored plants, such as the neon pink rose 'American Pillars'. Despite this grand display of color and fragrance, it is the structure of the garden that makes Chatwood so charming.

In building her garden, Mrs. Watkins took her cues from the house, a late-eighteenth-century clapboard structure. The design is simple, with Colonial Revival–style

formal gardens. Low brick walls and hedges separate one garden room from another, with simple wooden gates of vertical pales; paths are brick in the formal gardens and turf elsewhere; ceilings are the sky or aged walnuts, hackberries, elms, and American ash. Simplicity reigns, to great effect. The spaces of Chatwood breathe as you progress through them. The lawn off the back of the house is bordered by a low boxwood hedge and spring ephemerals. A giant black walnut looming over the lawn makes a ceiling that casts a dappled light. From the lawn, you move on to the sanctuary, a semicircular garden backed by red cedars (a common native tree) with a huge border of pale roses in front, all underplanted with forget-me-nots.

Next, a succession of prim and trim formal rose gardens are connected by the main path, which is off-center along the north side of the formal gardens. Roses grow on pillars and over walls, with the clipped hedges of dwarf yaupon edging beds brimming with flowers. The formality of these gardens contrasts nicely with the casual nature of the lawn near the house, and the sanctuary and one-acre meadow north of the formal gardens. The spaces change in character and size, opening to sweeping views

◀ *At Heronswood in Kingston, Washington, a tracery of clipped European hornbeam defines the space, yet is not visually massive. The lettuce-leaf poppies and alliums look wonderful above the haze of bronze fennel. Clipped hedges are seldom used in American gardens, but if the plants are selected well they require a minimum of maintenance and are excellent backdrops.*

of the meadow and woods. Roses are what people remember as they leave Chatwood, but it is the simple spaces that hold them and form the setting that make the garden memorable.

Walls

A wall or a fence defines space and establishes boundaries, essential elements in the articulation of any garden, whether for practical or philosophical purposes. Historically, fences were used to control the movement of people and/or animals, rather than to achieve an aesthetic effect. We may want a barrier between us and the rest of the world, to create a haven. We may wish to keep our children or pets in, safe from harm, or protect our property from damage by keeping animals or people out. Walls and fences also enable us to organize a large space into smaller areas with specific themes and uses.

For a garden maker, it is essential to address practical needs first. Having done so, the world expands quickly to a host of possibilities. I can hardly think of a garden I have designed that did not have a wall or fence. Even one of my smallest projects, a roof terrace twenty feet by twenty feet, included an arborvitae hedge, a living fence that screens out

▶ *The yew hedges in Piet Oudolf's garden in the Netherlands are wonderfully fluid, and light plays on them in magical ways. Yew is a perfect hedging plant because it needs clipping only once a year, and the black-green foliage is the perfect foil for most plants.*

nearby neighbors. Piet Oudolf uses yew hedges in his garden in the Netherlands. He plants traditional material in layers at the end of his garden, and lets the top undulate in a pattern that is dynamic with movement.

I lump fences into two very broad categories: fence as foreground and fence as backdrop. Low or transparent fences act as foreground, organizing a scene into visually digestible pieces and creating an edge to define a space and physically link it to larger landscape elements, such as pastoral views, or structures, such as houses, pavilions, or toolsheds. Architectural styles strengthen these ties: a picket fence with a Colonial Revival house, for example, or a wrought-iron fence with a Victorian gingerbread house. The quintessential American garden fence, made of wood pickets or pales, conjures visions of Americana and wholesomeness, which in turn effect a comforting nostalgia. Generally, hedges are less expensive, but they also contribute less to style. Built architecture is inherently more versatile.

It is not often that we see a pure slice of period aesthetics, because it takes passion and compulsion to thoroughly learn and replicate the physical hallmarks of a particular style. We are a society that likes to beg, borrow, and steal from a variety of traditions, so our homes and gardens are amalgams of style. I am thinking of a garden on Queen Anne Hill in Seattle, Washington, that is wildly

▶ *Walls can be permeable, like these designed by Steven Martino. They are visually potent, due to their form, and clearly define the outer perimeter of the garden.*

beautiful, obsessively excessive, and a pure slice of Victoriana (pages 90–91). Brian Coleman and Howard Cohen took a nondescript box and, over the course of fifteen years, turned it into Victorian gingerbread, complete with a frenetic garden that simultaneously repels and intrigues the visitor. The house is small and set back about twenty-five feet from the street. The front garden is a stage for the house: it is separated from the public space of the

▲ *Traditional construction materials can be used in nontraditional ways. These tongue-and-groove fences slide past one another on the diagonal. The back fence is painted a darker cobalt to enhance the sense of depth.*

▶ *The white-painted cap of this fence matches the white trim on the wood frame house. It is a definitely stated boundary: there is no doubt where it stops.*

street and sidewalk by a wrought-iron fence, backed by a clipped boxwood hedge. The house is covered with intricately carved bric-a-brac and is painted in contrasting saturated colors. The garden is one of the few I know that accurately reflect the period. The plants are not period, but their combinations are evocative of it. Glenn Withey and Charles Price, local garden designers, managed to outdo themselves and sate the client's appetite for the grotesquely beautiful. The slight incline from the sidewalk is planted with richly colored mahogany red and cream Gavota tulips, underplanted with orange and blue pansies. In the summer, the bed is planted with colored foliage, such as coleus and summer-flowering annuals.

Wooden fences require repair on a semiregular basis. Wood lasts between ten and twenty years if left unpainted, much longer if painted, depending on the quality and type

of wood used. Masonry walls and fences, though considerably more expensive, last a lifetime. An old friend in north-central New Jersey made beautiful use of old stone barn walls to define and shape her garden. They are a lovely backdrop to the setting of rolling grass meadows. She uses restraint and does not cover the walls completely so that they can be fully appreciated. Another advantage of masonry walls is that you can grow clinging vines—such as climbing hydrangea, Boston ivy, or English ivy—on them without compromising the structure. Never use clinging vines on a wooden structure, however, because the roots trap moisture and cause rot. On wooden fences, use twining vines such as clematis, roses, and morning glories.

I have been discussing more traditional fences and planting styles, but gardens with a more modern perspective are in vogue. In my client Graeme Hardie's garden in Nutley, New Jersey, we used clapboard siding to build the walls that surround his fifty-foot-by-fifty-foot garden. The clapboard is the same as that on the house, a strong connection to the architecture we intended. In the main fence separating the driveway from the garden, the horizontal clapboard creates a rhythm of lines across changing elevation, seven feet from the main terrace to the lowest point in the garden. The boards follow the grade and are on the diagonal, creating a strong sense of movement and drama (page 46).

Linda Cochran of Bainbridge Island, Washington, loves color, and the stucco walls of her garden are inspired by her time living in the Southwest. Like Graeme, she has gone for blue, but hers is a less saturated color, and complementary rather than contrasting. The variegated *Miscanthus sinensis* 'Cosmopolitan' lightens up the scene even more. Its white color and finer texture contrast dramatically with the Abyssinian banana, *Ensete ventricosum* 'Maurelii'. The self-sowing annual *Verbena bonariensis* adds a light-hearted touch of lavender. On the other end of the wall, the dark-leafed *Dahlia* 'Fascination' is a shock of pink that will brighten any cloudy day in the Pacific Northwest.

I have spent my life gardening in a temperate climate, but I would love to garden in the desert. The austerity of that environment and the sculptural quality of its plants lend themselves naturally to a minimalist approach. In April 2000, I went to Phoenix, Arizona, to see the work of master garden maker Steve Martino. His use of garden architecture complements the qualities of the plants that have adapted to this harsh climate. Steven uses a rich variety of walls to separate, confine, and focus space, along with an array of building materials, which he uses with knowing flair. The first garden of his I saw was at a wholesale nursery called Arid Zone Trees. At the entrance to the property, flanking the gate, are stucco walls. On the right, going in, are a series of impressive and cleanly simple forms, where the play of light is exquisite. On the left, a zigzag wall creates captivating shadows.

◀ Serpentine walls were a favorite of Thomas Jefferson and his contemporaries because they used less material and were structurally very sound. Here they provide a strong backdrop to the plantings in a less than ordinary way.

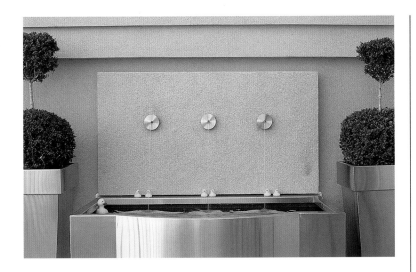

The plantings are simple: a ground cover of California poppies, a cactus or two, and blue agaves. I was expecting an overly masculine landscape filled with saguaro cacti, which are pervasive in our notion of the desert. In the front garden, the major features are ingeniously conceived and beautifully executed walls. The main walk to the administration building slices through the landscape. Entering from the parking lot at midlength, the walk terminates in the garden in a small-scaled amphitheater-like space. The terminus to the walk and focus of the space is

---

▲ *This stainless steel fountain, with flanking planters, is clean and crisp. The raised panel adds relief to the building wall. The panel is offset from the wall two inches, allowing easy access to the plumbing for the fountainheads.*

◄ *Concrete blocks are thought of as utilitarian, but here they have a bold elegance that goes beyond function. The wriggling low wall covered in green glass tiles is a beautiful sculptural element in the composition.*

a concrete plinth, with a potted agave sitting on it. Low concrete-block benches ripple out like concentric wavelets in a pond.

The wall that surrounds the terminal space is made of concrete squares and what I suspect are chimney flues. The pattern is wonderfully graphic and soothing. The spiky forms of several *Yucca rostrata* punctuate the space with their steel-gray leaves. Heading back toward the building, a serpentine sunset orange stucco wall is planted with a row of acacia. The simple rhythm of the trees, which structures and punctuates the back-and-forth movement of the wall, is at once logical and playful. The underplanting, with salvias and *Sphaeralcea ambigua*, is soft and scrubby. One plant stands out. Near the end of the wall, by the parking lot, is a Medusa-like agave. The plant's sensuously curving leaves are brilliant and dramatic against the stark form of the wall (page 14).

The back garden contains several smaller spaces, again with concrete-block walls in a variety of shapes, styles, and patterns. The most striking is a series of forms at the back of the garden that resemble plum-colored shark fins slicing through the desert floor (pages 44–45). The foreground to these bizarre structures is a tapestry of gray-leafed plants, such as brittlebush, *Encelia farinosa*, and *Opuntia violacea*. The image of silver and purple plants set against the purple wall inspires me every time I recall it.

In a private garden in Scottsdale, Arizona, Steve was no less innovative. The walls are all of stucco, most of them a dull taupe that blends in with the brown foothills in the distance. At the entrance, a clean lemon-colored

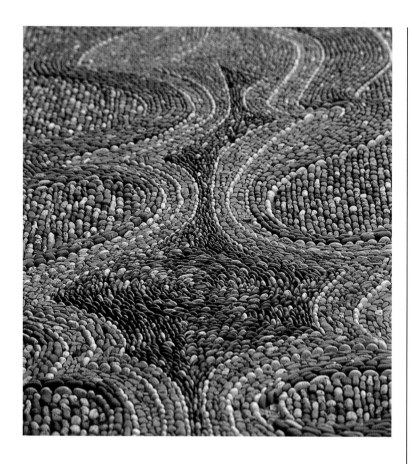

garden. Aside from walls and fences, how we treat the floor will define how the garden is organized and used. There must be enough open space to serve the people living in the garden. Obvious needs, such as getting from the street to the entrance of the home, will determine how much surface to pave and how paved areas will relate to the architecture and reach beyond into the garden.

Paved surfaces are more expensive but easier to walk on and maintain; most important, they provide focus to activities that take place in the garden. Paths connect these spaces, one to another. When thinking about paved surfaces, there are several important points to remember. Their proportions should be generous enough to be comfortably usable. Bold shapes are more effective than small, poorly articulated ones, and paths should be laid out logically and in broad strokes.

One of the biggest failures in a garden is a network of paths that meander with no intent or perceived destination. Paths should relate to the house, and strong focal

low wall is lovely in morning light, set off by a skirt of *Sphaeralcea ambigua* backed by palo verde, *Cercidium floridum* (page 27). At the front entrance, a large burnt red stucco wall links guest quarters to the main residence. The red vibrates: it is a staggering backdrop for Otatea, *Fouquieria splendens*, agaves, and more palo verde. It is a stage, with indigenous plants as the players.

Floors

The ground plane and how we treat it figure as one of the most significant elements we can manipulate in the garden. Paths, terraces, and planting beds give shape to the

points will make them most effective. Main paths should be wide enough—usually four or five feet—to accommodate two people with ease. Depending on the scale of the site and existing architecture, they can be even wider. Secondary paths can be smaller—three feet is comfortable, but a path narrower than that increases tension and lessens ease of movement. Beginning gardeners often make their paths too narrow, thinking they are saving space for plants and other uses. The result, however, is a garden that is not easy to navigate and feels cramped.

Paths with straight lines give a sense of formality and a high degree of structure. Curved lines are less formal and more casual. Be careful that curves are not too tight but large and gracious. Lots of squiggles in a path are distracting, unsettling, and may seem random. Curves fit better if they take into account the contours of the site.

Changes in elevation give variety and impact to flat sites and are a necessity on slopes. For gentle grades, ramping is a nice way to proceed from one level to another. For steeper slopes, stairs are the most efficient way to change levels. Risers four to five inches high are most comfortable if space is limited. For more severe grades, six-inch risers should be considered a maximum for outdoor steps. In the steepest locations, switchbacks may be required. Remember that flat space is necessary for centers of activity, such as terraces and play space for children. There is nothing more unsettling than feeling as if you are sliding downhill.

Paving materials range from man-made to natural, formal to casual. Stone is often the most costly, but adds

atmosphere and the patina of age to a garden. Cut stones—such as bluestone, sandstone, limestone, and granite—work best in highly architectural settings, whereas random-shaped stones are more informal. Paving patterns should be simple and straightforward. Bricks are adaptable to both formal and informal uses, depending on how they are laid. Gravel generally adds a casual feel to the garden and, though inexpensive, is more time consuming to keep weeded and tidy. Gravel is most effective and easier to maintain if it has a clearly defined edge of metal, stone, or brick. Concrete, which is considered a modern material, has actually been used since the Romans dominated the ancient world. Today, concrete can be colored, imprinted with textural patterns, or finished with aggregates. It need not be boring, and its fluid nature allows for patterns that are not possible with modular paving materials.

Terraces, patios, and decks are entertainment spaces. They are frequently associated with the kitchen for convenience, but should also be connected to a home's public spaces, such as the dining and living rooms. Paved surfaces work best for these floors, rather than lawn, because they can accommodate heavy traffic and support furniture. The size of a terrace should relate to the scale of the house

◀ *The arbor over the work area and driveway and across the front of the house at Little and Lewis Studio, on Bainbridge Island, Washington, gives continuity to the garden. The rambunctious 'Paul's Himalayan' musk rose is a show-stopper in full flower, covering the arbor in what looks like pale pink soapsuds.*

and its intended use. For instance, a couple that does not entertain will require less paved surface than a family that entertains large numbers of people. Large paved areas can be broken up with planting beds and arbors. As with the width of a garden path, here is a place to plan for more space than you think you might need.

I love plants, but I don't think the entire garden should be given over to them. Paved surfaces are essential

---

▲ This arbor, based on classical ideas, is playfully adapted with saturated blue and turquoise and modern construction materials, including concrete posts.

◀ A pergola is an abstract conceit of a tree grove. This one, laden with wisteria, was designed by turn-of-the-century landscape architect Beatrix Ferrand at Old Westbury, New York. This vine has a romantic look, but it grows very vigorously and needs hours of proper pruning and training to look its best. If neglected, it can also do considerable damage to architectural structures.

to establish a solid frame for the garden and to ensure the garden is usable. After all, the garden is a place to live in. Planning for the many and varied functions of that living space is essential.

Ceilings

Walls and plantings define the vertical edges of a garden, and lowering the ceiling is another effective way to increase intimacy. When we stand in the middle of an open field, the expanse makes us feel exposed and the wide-open sky makes us feel small. We can increase our sense of security by shrinking the dimensions of the space to a more human level.

Trees are the most common ceilings in any garden. We plant them for shade and to modulate the space of the garden. Large trees, such as oaks or maples, evoke a different feeling than medium or small ones. The size of the trees you plant will depend on the scale of the property. If you have a half acre or more—and lots of patience—you might choose a pin oak or honey locust. They grow very large and will provide a sense of permanence to a garden. Large old trees are comforting; they impart a sense of timeless continuity, and they are worth preserving. A good arborist can shape and thin your grand trees so that their branch structure can be appreciated and to ensure that enough light penetrates so that the ground beneath isn't too shaded.

Trees take a long time to realize their potential size, and they change the character of a garden more than

other plants. For this reason, we respect their presence in the garden. Just give a friend an impatiens and an oak seedling in four-inch pots and watch the reaction. We all know the impatiens is an annual and affects the garden for only a few months. The oak, on the other hand, connotes permanence, age, process, and commitment. In our mobile society, many people don't think planting a large tree is worth doing because they will never see it mature. Crabapples, dogwoods, and crepe myrtles are easier to consider because they are smaller, so their size at maturity seems more attainable. Given the opportunity, I plant both sizes. I get the immediate satisfaction of seeing the small-scale trees mature, cast their shade, and define the space. At the same time, I can imagine the

This arbor is over an outdoor dining and entertaining area of a home in Scottsdale, Arizona. The open metal roof complements the spare architecture of the house and is quite dense, providing plenty of shade in this hot, sunny climate.

majesty that a climax tree will someday impart, whether I am there to enjoy it or not.

Canopy density and leaf size and shape affect the shadiness or transparency of the ceiling. Honey locusts are popular trees because they grow fast, and their small leaflets create bright shade that does not feel dank and gloomy. Red maples also grow fast, but their large leaves and dense canopy allow little light to reach the ground. I never use them in residential gardens because they are not generous neighbors to other plants. They have an extremely competitive root system, which can extract all water and nutrients from the surrounding soil. That, coupled with lack of light, means that only a few stalwart plants are able to grow near them.

Arbors, pergolas, lath houses, and lanais are man-made abstractions of tree canopies that can be used where trees are inappropriate or are unwanted. The advantages of these structures are that they provide strong links to the house, their shade is easily moderated depending on the spacing of the rafters, the variety of possible construction materials and styles makes them adaptable to any garden, and their impact is immediate. Vines are often coupled with these structures but tend to be overused. I prefer arbors that are clean, open, and display the builder's craftsmanship. Vines on arbors are loveliest when they are just a tracery, allowing plenty of sun to reach the floor. Too often, a vigorous vine is planted at the base of the structure and within several years is too dense, obliterating the sun and smothering the structure. Wisteria is the worst offender. This vise-grip plant is rarely trained properly. It is allowed to scramble hither and yon like an errant child, when it should be pruned ruthlessly. Once tamed, it should be kept firmly in check with regular trimming. A strong and muscular plant, wisteria will tear apart built structures with ease if neglected.

Lath houses, which are structures made of spaced strips of wood through which sun penetrates, can be great additions to the garden. They are usually larger structures, which should assume or reflect the outline of the site's dominant architecture. The most beautiful one I know is at Montrose in Hillsborough, North Carolina, where the lath house in the center of the garden mimics the silhouettes of the eighteenth-century barns on the property. Nancy Goodwin grows her choicest shade plants in this lovely setting, which provides the advantages of proper light without root competition from trees.

Lowering the ceiling, whether with architecture or trees, creates places in the garden that offer comfort and a sense of security. Places to stop, rest, and soak in the scene around you. ■

Sequence and Progression

She went down the path

and through the second green door.

There she found more walls

and winter vegetables and glass frames,

but in the second wall there was

another green door and it was not open.

Perhaps it led into the garden

no one had seen in ten years.

~

FRANCES HODGSON BURNETT,

The Secret Garden

This deck in Graeme Hardie's lower garden in Nutley, New Jersey, disguises a hot tub. A hatch in the deck lifts to provide access to a soothing dip. A pot filled with summer annuals sits on the bluestone plinth, providing a focal point from the main terrace and the walk through the lower garden.

◄ *This fresh-looking tender fountain grass,* **Pennisetum setaceum** *'Purpureum', blooms all summer long. It is planted with* **Scaevola aemula** *'Blue Wonder', and the fresh green of asparagus fern, which contrasts with the dark purple.*

▶ *The view down this hallway from the breakfast nook is focused on* Arrow, *a sculpture by Nicholas Morden. The fastigiate boxwoods further frame the view, and the yellow* **Acorus gramineus** *'Ogon' is striking against the blue wall screening out the drive.*

I've talked a lot about what fills a garden, but a garden is about empty space as well—the place where we live, the place we move through. And that space in a landscape is shaped by certain expectations. Some sort of entry is required. If the garden is in front of the home, we assume we will be led to the front door. A back garden is usually where we live, thus it will likely have areas for different functions, which depend on the needs of the household.

When I began designing a garden for my friend and client Graeme Hardie, I had already known him for six years or so. Our history and familiarity gave me important insight into his needs for the new garden. I knew how he lived, what his leisure activities were, what his aesthetic sense was. I knew he would want room for sculptures, ample space for entertaining, and lots of flowers. He would need privacy so the garden felt comfortable and secure. He asked for a hot tub, and he wanted the garden to be exuberant and junglelike. There were drainage problems, drastic changes in elevation, and the geometry of a breakfast nook jutting from the back of the house. All of these

issues had to be reconciled in a space that was approximately fifty feet square.

The architect Henry Clark, who designed the home's renovation, left me with a large brick and bluestone terrace, raised some five feet above the lowest part of the garden. The terrace is connected to the sun porch and deck, which are connected to the foyer. From the foyer, one can see through to the back garden looking straight ahead, and to the right the kitchen and beyond it the terrace. Henry also designed a lovely garage with a colonnade alongside that faces the garden.

I wanted to make a garden that would hold a variety of experiences, even in such a small space. I planned a circular route through the garden, beginning and ending back at the foyer. The route reflects the geometry of the house, which sits square on the property, and the breakfast nook, which was an addition and introduced a new geometry based on thirty- and sixty-degree angles. The layout unites the two features into a more harmonious

whole. First, I established a strong view through the wall of windows from the breakfast tables. A path of large granite cobble stepping pads set in a basket-weave pattern leads to the focal point, a plinth or pedestal holding a piece of sculpture. This narrow, strongly focused space formed a hallway to what would become the lower garden.

Next, I focused on the main terrace. Henry had done a fine job of linking the house to what would become the main living and entertaining space. Now I would need to add stairs and additional terraces to hold the hot tub and lead to the rear of the garden. I designed another hallway along the edge of the property line, perpendicular to the back of the house. It would descend four or so steps down to a lower seating area just large enough for two chairs. I like to think of spaces as breathing—the large terrace would constrict to a hall and widen slightly near the seating area.

> I wanted to make a garden that would hold a variety of experiences, even in such a small space.
>
> ✤

From the seating area I wanted a hallway to connect to a lower deck that would hold the hot tub and connect visually with the lower garden. This deck is probably about ten feet across in each direction, with the main view turning from the house and focused on the same pedestal and sculpture that you can see from the breakfast nook. We would need a four-foot retaining wall to hold back the slope, which runs parallel to the back of the house and the colonnade next to the garage. There were now major spaces: the main terrace, the lower garden, what would become the largest planted area in the garden, and major views from the house. Secondary spaces included the seating area for two, and the deck with sunken hot tub. A visitor to the garden can take a little journey before or after dinner.

We planted the main garden with large-scale plants intended to overwhelm the visitor—Graeme's idea for the

◄ From the third-floor guest bedroom you can look down on the garden and get a sense of the circular path around the garden. The colonnade along the garage face makes it an attractive asset to the garden, rather than a visual liability. You are looking into the main planting area, which is planted with large-scale perennials that are intended to be lush and junglelike.

▶ The graciousness of the main terrace allows plenty of space to entertain a party of four or twenty, as Graeme does regularly when the weather allows. The blue-and-yellow Moroccan table inspired the same color scheme in the plantings throughout the garden.

jungle. The lower garden would be planted with ground cover, punctuated with grasses and a few large-leafed tropical plants, such as elephant ears, on either end. I wanted this space to contrast with the area closer to the house and feel open to the sky. The paths themselves became important to distinguish the different areas. The walk that connects the garden to the driveway is brick, edged in bluestone like the terrace, but the stepping pads

are granite. The walk in the lower garden is paved with Mexican river gravel, held in place by granite cobble edging. I wanted this to feel good on your feet as you came out of the hot tub, in contrast to all the other hard surfaces. The walk connecting the main terrace to the seating area and the small terrace itself is again brick with bluestone trim. Finally, the deck surrounding the hot tub relates back to the deck across the back of the house,

◀ The captivating variegated devil's walking stick will get better with the years, reaching an ultimate height of ten feet or so. The stick man in the foreground animates and personalizes the space. Graeme brought it home from a trip to South Africa, his homeland, making it a much-loved personal statement for him.

◀◀ Arundo donax, giant reed grass, screens the lower garden from the stairs leading to the kitchen and back deck. Watching the grass emerge and grow to nearly twenty feet in a single growing season is like watching performance art.

connecting the breakfast nook with the doors from the foyer to the large terrace.

Walls border two sides of the garden: the house and the garage provide privacy on the other two. The walls are built of materials that complement the architecture, but are painted a daring and unexpected three shades of blue. The blue works well with the conservative gray house and white trim, but is

buoyant and childlike, making the garden seem even more like a fantasy unto itself. Pots, furniture, and sculpture add drama and texture to the garden. I tried to make the design a united whole that is livable and richly beautiful.

I can describe this garden, show you pictures, but to know it you must walk through it and experience the modulation of spaces: feel the hard brick and granite underfoot turn to soft crunchy gravel, see the lushness of the plants, feel the vegetation encroaching and looming overhead. The most exciting thing about gardens is the space they create—how we can move through them and how they affect the way we feel.

If a site has expansive views, preserve and frame them. Add small domestic garden rooms near the house that will offer respite and a place to just sit and enjoy. Each feature of the garden should relate to, enhance, and complement the next to create a place of variety and satisfaction, while forming a satisfying whole. ■

Scale

Only people and cats stay the same size

indoors and out. A house chair on the lawn

dwindles and looks overdressed.

The daintiest lilac bush in the garden

would be a white elephant in the parlor.

Magic gets in somehow and changes the size

of any object as it goes through the garden door.

~

FLETCHER STEELE,

Gardens and People

*Sissinghurst is an English gardening icon. The gardens
were a collaboration between Harold Nicholson and his wife,
Vita Sackville-West. Harold loved structure and organized the
framework of the garden, while Vita planted it masterfully in
a naturalistic romantic spirit. Though the garden is nearly
three acres, it is carved into smaller spaces that are
comfortable in scale.*

Scale is a hard concept to grasp. We relate the size of objects and spaces to the human form and, more specifically, our own size. How big is big? It is most important to begin with the size of the space you are dealing with. If it is large, are you going to carve it into smaller spaces? The size of your garden may be predetermined if you are an urban dweller—a small yard or even a terrace. When starting with a small area, do not be tempted to cut it up into smaller spaces. You'll need enough room to move around comfortably. Also, planters, architectural features, and the plants themselves should be large enough to relate to the architecture.

I have seen gardens with limited space in which the owner has made the paths, seating areas, and features diminutive. This approach makes you feel like Gulliver in the land of the Lilliputians. It is rare, but possible, to make things too large; it is very easy to make things too small. I know of a garden in the Southeast whose owners thought it would be cute to make their garden three-quarter scale. If you are a child, standing in this garden feels great. For the rest of us, it feels bizarre, too small and cramped, as if you have outgrown your skin.

When presented with a small space, be clearheaded about your concept. Clients of mine in Seattle have a penthouse condominium with a spacious L-shaped terrace with sweeping views east across Lake Washington. The largest area projects from the living room to the water, and a long, narrow section runs in front of the master bedroom. The interior décor is eclectic: lovely classical furniture

contrasts with modern pieces and a great collection of contemporary art. Custom-built traditional planters containing large plants are strategically placed to screen views of the neighbors. Camellias, intended to be maintained

▲ *Fastigiate Irish yews give focus and structure to the blowsy perennial planting in the warm color scheme of the sunset garden at Sissinghurst.*

◄ *Spires of verbascum, ligularia, and Maltese cross complement and contrast in a masterful combination of plants.*

at seven feet or so, and three rectangular planters (about eighteen inches high, eighteen inches wide, and four feet long) containing clipped boxwood hedges define the space further and focus the visitor on the main view. The largest planter, a four-foot cube, has a large Japanese maple that hints of an overhead. All the wooden boxes are raised-panel construction and painted a high-gloss dove gray.

The main view is framed by two large, black cast-iron planters finished with silver highlights. They are planted with colored annuals, using mostly reds or whites for a classic look. The garden furniture is cream-colored woven plastic, with a marble table on a cast-iron base. The long, narrow portion of the terrace leading to the master bedroom was a problem because it ended at a blank wall. I designed a fountain with flanking planters in a traditional form, but made of stainless steel, that contain double-ball boxwood topiaries (page 51).

We limited our scope, took cues from the interior by contrasting classical and modern elements, and didn't fill the space. The terrace is comfortable and beautiful, and each element is appropriately sized to relate to the building. Too often we get greedy and stuff small spaces to overflowing, which only makes them cramped.

I confess I like large-scale items in the garden—large plants or containers in a space make for grand theatrical gestures. Graeme Hardie's blue-walled garden in New Jersey has giant reed grass, *Arundo donax*, that grows to nearly twenty feet in a growing season. The grass is like performance art: it grows so fast it changes the whole feeling of the garden as it grows. It starts at ground level each spring, and by September looms high over the privacy fence against the backdrop of the three-story house. In this case,

the grass is intended to overwhelm. Cannas are used extensively in his garden for the same reason; they are large, overscaled, and tropical.

Silas Mountsier's garden, across the street from Graeme's, is about an acre in area, so there is more room to play with. Views are important to Silas, so we took advantage of the length of the property to make them as extensive as possible. Two long lawns are parallel, but separated by midsize trees (eastern dogwoods, stewartias,

and pond cypress) and larger shrubs such as bamboo and viburnums. The garden is a place to display Silas's collection of garden art. Smaller-scaled spaces connect the two lawns. You enter through a circular brick wall, configured much like a chambered nautilus shell, and move to the other large lawn through a door in the opposite side of the shell. At the other end, off the main terrace, a smaller square terrace is superimposed on a circular garden pool. Just big enough for two people, the tiny terrace is an intimate space that provides relief from the larger areas.

When you have enough room to divide into smaller areas, modulate the spaces dramatically. Make the big as big as you comfortably can, but contrast the large space with a small garden that comfortably holds just a few people. The key word is comfort. Even small areas should feel gracious.

Individual elements should be appropriately scaled as well. The hanging pyramid containers at the Washington Park Arboretum in Seattle (pages 124–125) were made large because the arbor they hang from is large. The posts that support it are massive, twelve by twelve inches, with two-by-twelve-inch structural boards on top. Arbors constructed with the more common four-inch-square posts are generally too small to relate properly to most people's

homes; six- or eight-inch-square posts work better. Smaller posts fit well with a really small house with a tiny yard.

Sissinghurst Castle in Kent, England, is the site of the spectacular gardens created by Harold Nicholson and his wife, the writer Vita Sackville-West. Sissinghurst is the quintessential English flower garden. Vita's lush romantic planting style and her incredible use of color charms many gardeners' hearts, but it is Harold who deserves much of the credit. It was he who planted the hedges, creating sight lines and vistas that made the spaces to hold Vita's floral abundance. This is the real reason so many people love Sissinghurst—they relate to the smaller scale of the individual gardens, even though the entire garden covers nearly three acres! Each smaller theme garden—the famous white garden,

sunset garden, rose garden, and others—can be experienced as a self-contained and lovely garden unto itself.

The antithesis of Sissinghurst is the Kandall Sculpture Garden at PepsiCo in Purchase, New York, designed by Russell Page, the great landscape architect who practiced from the early 1930s until his death in 1985. The Kandall

▲ This Alexander Calder sculpture at PepsiCo, the corporate headquarters of Pepsi Cola in Purchase, New York, is dwarfed by the parklike setting. No sense of scale could be perceived if it weren't for the people in the photograph.

▶ Windows define a view and make a large world more accessible by shrinking it and limiting the available visual information.

Garden is parklike in scale, with a golden path that circumnavigates the property. The garden celebrates great contemporary sculptors on a monolithic scale. An Alexander Calder sculpture, some thirty feet tall and set against a grove of mature Himalayan pines and blue firs, dwarfs the visitor.

Not many of us get to play with a large canvas like PepsiCo's grounds. The key is to make the most of what you have without being greedy and cramming too much into any space, no matter how large or small. Make each

▶ *These rustic pots gain impact from their large size and impose themselves into the space. They would look ridiculous if they were smaller, because they would lack presence against this expanse of wall.*

element—walks, walls, trees, benches—relate to the space and to each other. Be consistent, but, most of all, think graciousness and comfort. ■

Time

June came late that year,

almost July, almost not at all.

I thought they would never come

those June days all white and blue and warm,

whose greens are still young enough

to be blue and chartreuse;

warm fragrant days

like the herald flowers of the month, roses.

~

ROBERT DASH,

Notes from Madoo

The abundance of June has arrived at the Northwest Perennial Alliance border at the Bellevue Botanical Garden in Bellevue, Washington. Greens are still lush and fresh, and the large-scale grasses are making themselves known, creating wonderful undulations of mass and void in the border.

Measuring time can be one of those depressing acts in your life—no matter how fulfilled you are, you can always use more. When we first build and plant a new garden or bed, we want to see the garden with the mossy patina of age and all the plants grown to that perfect stage of life, the one in the mind's eye when the garden was first envisioned. I dream about gardens (all the time, in fact) and about what can be. If I'm lucky, the visions are approximate; if I'm even luckier, the reality is better than what I imagined.

I remember visiting a locally prominent nurseryman in my hometown, Crestwood, Kentucky, on a visit home from college. Theodore Kline was in his middle eighties then. It was autumn, and I found him at the potting bench sowing fastigiate English oak acorns in large community flats. I was struck by the faith of this act. What was this man thinking, planting acorns at his age? Yet he was doing the same thing he had done every fall most of his working life, knowing that one day these trees would be tall and majestic no matter who was there to see them. The point is, someone

It is difficult to live in the moment in a garden because we are so used to anticipation.

would see them. You accept that you may never live to see an oak reach maturity or a giant redwood reach middle age and exert its presence over your garden, but you plant them knowing someone long after you will be there to witness your act of faith.

Annuals require little patience—six weeks' worth at best. They are fun and fast, and that is why they hold such appeal. Gardening and time, no matter how much money you spend to buy the biggest plants you can find, are inextricable. Even when you plant the largest trees and the largest perennials, it is time that allows everything to settle together as a single fabric. The rawness of a new garden can only be smoothed out over the course of months and years.

Living with a garden day to day and year to year is one of the great simple pleasures of my life, although I do not have a garden at home. For now, the Elisabeth C. Miller

◀ *In October, though the zenith of the border is past, the fall color of the shrubs offers subtle relief from the exuberance of summer.*

▶ *Time to tidy up. Cutting back the garden in winter, and then manuring it, will ready it for the next growing season. Hordes of volunteers keep this mixed border in tip-top shape year round.*

Botanical Garden is where I mark my time. It is a luxury to know where the sun falls at various times of day: when I come to work, the Olympic Mountains are cast in a rosy light on a clear morning, and at the end of the day they are silhouetted against the western sun. Taking pictures makes me acutely aware of how the sun moves through the garden, and teaches me to savor the light at 10:00 A.M. on the pale pink flowers of Rhododendron pseudochrysanthum in the upper woods or the tulips in large containers on the library terrace backlit by the late afternoon sun.

Bulbs represent another kind of gardening optimism— here is a wizened time capsule that will miraculously metamorphose into an explosion of color and life. When bulbs arrive in plant stores in late autumn, they are hard and turgid, with a papery skin. I can't help but finger them: the curve of a tulip, the garliclike cloves of giant alliums (my favorite is 'Globe Master'), the long neck of a daffodil. Each is a slightly different shape and size, variations on a theme. In late October, planting bulbs, my mind wanders to February's crocuses, March's daffodils, April's tulips, and May's alliums.

It is difficult to live in the moment in a garden, because we are so used to anticipation. When the alliums emerge in early March, the strappy leaves look fresh and stiff. That state doesn't last long. The leaves lose their luster by mid-April, when the minarets of flower buds start to make their presence known. They reach skyward as the foliage goes into decline. By late April, 'Globe Master' is twenty-four inches tall and not yet finished. Apple green stems and buds rocket from the earth. May is even more wrought with anticipation. The buds grow larger as the leaves begin to shrivel. By the middle of the month, the buds are transformed into softball-size heads of millions of starry purple flowers—a living sculpture that materializes before our eyes.

Of course, a garden is made up of many plants, so we watch these annual cycles play out, one after another, all around us—rosebuds fattening and opening, sunflowers asserting themselves, the first leaf turning color in September and building to a crescendo in October and November, and the first frost, when the garden is stripped bare. In February, the smell of just-delivered manure brings us full circle.

Bulldozers are an exciting and terrifying sight at the same time—large, loud, and powerful. But to see the earth moved and re-formed is magic. As a garden is being built, I eagerly watch the working of each tradesman who comes and goes. A hole turns into a pool; a wall materializes where there was none; soil is worked and plants go in the ground. After the

▶ *Softball-size heads of millions of mauve flowers make me imagine each flower is a microcosm unto itself.*

◄ *Construction is nerve-wracking, chaotic, and usually takes twice as long as the contractors say it will. Nevertheless, it is exciting to see the form of a new garden emerge, evolving from the imagination into reality.*

▼ *This second photograph was taken four short months from the previous one. Look what a difference a little time makes. I long to see the trees mature and feel the impact they will have over this lovely place. This is the garden of Silas Mountsier, in Nutley, New Jersey. Silas appreciates time's influence on a garden. We have been working together for a decade now, always looking at the garden with a critical eye and fine-tuning it with each passing year.*

▲ *Tulips are the great extravagance of Si's garden. Each fall we plant about 2,000 of them, then celebrate spring with parties for the ten days they are in flower. If May is cool, the tulips last longer. A blast of unexpected heat will shorten their flowering time.*

weeks of planning and months of construction, comes the reward, one of the pinnacles of gardening for me. When everyone is gone and the new garden is quiet—no more pounding or rumbling of equipment—then all there is to do is wait, wait and see if time will realize what the imagination conjured.

Good gardens take lots of time—years and years for trees to grow tall enough to cast shade, hedges to separate intended rooms, borders to fill in with a lush spectacle. When the plants start to fail, the gardener intercedes to fill in holes, prune to allow sun where it has been blotted out, look with fresh eyes to see what time has accomplished, and guess what will come next in order to correct mistakes and keep the vision on course.

I look back and remember gardens that I have built, and know that in my short career they are already gone. I hope that the trees I planted are growing and will one day be the beautiful grove of cherries on the hillside I envisioned. That the 'Hazel Smith' giant redwoods will be the impressive backdrop to the cherries, as intended. That the 36,000 daffodils will grow into larger clumps with each passing year. That people will appreciate these things, which will make the waiting worthwhile. And—like Mr. Kline—that I will never give up on gardens of the future. ■

▼ *These beds—decked out in coleus, impatiens, and African palm grass,* Setaria palmifolia *'Rubra', for textural relief—look great in late June, but are at their best in July, August, and September. In late October, after a killing frost, these summer annuals go on the compost heap, and tulips are overplanted with dozens of flowering cabbages.*

Color

They walked along listening to the singing of
brightly colored birds and looking at the lovely
flowers which now became so thick the ground
was carpeted with them.
There were big yellow and white and blue
and purple blossoms, besides the great clusters
of scarlet poppies, which were so brilliant
in color they almost dazzled Dorothy's eyes.

~

L. FRANK BAUM,

The Wonderful Wizard of Oz

Christopher Lloyd never fails to be a provocateur. Here in the
long border at Great Dixter, pink phlox and tamerisk collide
with an orange Crocosmia 'Firebrand' and Knifophia
unvaria 'Nobilis', and are tempered with plum purple Salvia
nemerosa and old gold Helenium.

◄ The statuesque crown imperials, Fritillaria imperialis, are stunning with the purple rhododendrons, and the variegated ivy is a perfect highlight with the forest green house. The mustard columns dominate because of their relative visual mass; even though the yellow crown imperial is brighter, it is considerably smaller.

▶ Brian Coleman and Howard Cohen have created a Victorian fantasy on Queen Anne Hill in Seattle, Washington. The house and the garden, designed by Glenn Withey and Charles Price, though extremely complex, are bedecked with muted shades of green, yellow, and red. The effect is rich and overwhelming. Less intense colors do not lessen the impact here.

Color is one of the most alluring aspects of gardening. We all have some basic understanding of color and how it works, and it can bring out childlike playfulness in each of us. It can be demure, dynamic, playful, or explosive. It can also be quiet, staid, or even morose. I began to learn about color in college, when my good friend Alan Cavelarro introduced me to the subject in a methodical way. At the time, Alan was a textile design student and already an accomplished painter. I had just returned from my first trip to England with some 600 slides of gardens. I was a fan of Gertrude Jekyll's and William Robinson's ideas about the naturalistic style of planting; design and color play important roles in their theories. With many new ideas floating around in my head, I wanted to understand more about how others were manipulating color. I would load up several carousels of slides, invite Alan over, and we would review each one, talking for hours about his impressions of the colors in the images. It helped that he knew nothing about plants and little about gardening. He was unbiased and could see the images with a fresh perspective. I could learn about color without getting caught up in which plants were being used, and whether they would or would not grow in Raleigh, North Carolina, where I was living at the time.

Color is essential to my life. My living room is chartreuse, my dining room sunshine yellow, my bathroom turquoise, and the rest of the place—well, you get the

picture. I believe you can change your whole perspective on life with a trip to the paint store and a little elbow grease. My own bias is to use medium intensity and lots of color, which gives a buoyant, childlike effect. I have never been one to worry about getting the exact shade to paint this wall or adding that plant to a particular scheme.

▲ *This fresh blue-and-white color scheme at the E. B. Dunn Garden in Seattle would please even the most staunch traditionalist: Corydalis 'Blue Panda' with Anemone nemerosa 'Vesta' and grape hyacinths.*

▶ *Pastels are ethereal and were once nearly the only accepted scheme for flower gardens of sophisticated taste. This very modern garden by Piet Oudolf at his nursery and home in the Netherlands puts a new spin on pinks and mauves. The soft colors are made more frothy by using many fine-textured plants. The crooked spires of clipped weeping silver pear, Pyrus salicifolia 'Pedula', are striking structural notes but also soften the scheme with a large mass of silver.*

◄ The burnt orange of **Crocosmia 'Emily McKenzie'** *contrasts with* **Geranium wlassovianum.** *Reds are always effective in the garden because they are complements to green and intensify one another. Dark oranges have a strong but less potent effect.*

▶ The sumptuous golden orange trumpets of **Lilium 'African Queen'** *are stunning in July, when they tower six feet into the sky.*

I am only interested in relative values—how different hues and intensities work with each other, how magenta fights with chartreuse in an explosive combination that some people love and others hate, with little middle ground. Chartreuse is halfway between green and yellow on the color wheel, just as magenta is midway between violet and blue. The two colors thus are across from each other and therefore complementary—that is, they intensify each other. As red is the complement to green, and gardens are predominantly green, red livens up the garden pretty fast. I use this trick often in gardens that are mostly green. Green is familiar and soothing, so when I begin planning a new garden, I recognize we are most often looking for refuge from daily life. Everything else in the garden will relate to this basic and predominant underpinning of green.

My friend and client Silas Mountsier owns the garden I have worked on the longest at this point in my career. We have been working together for ten years now on an acre of ground. What we have done is a reflection of what he started in the early 1950s. I have tried to understand his likes and dislikes and distill them into a more powerful whole. This garden is built upon two basic tenets: the structure should be bold and broad (the garden is mostly curves derived from a terrace he installed in the 1960s), and it should serve as a fitting and quiet backdrop for the many pieces of sculpture Silas has collected and continues to collect. This last objective is why I used very few varie-

The light blue of the **Opuntia violacea** *is cool and soothing against this curved purple wall. The waxy coating is an adaptive characteristic of many desert plants to reflect the strong Southwest sun, but it can create icy images in the garden.*

gated plants in the garden. Green would be the dominant color, with lots of evergreens to provide structure during the winter. Color does play an important role, but for impact it is concentrated in strategic areas, such as the terminus of a view or the junction of major paths. Silas's Dutch Colonial home is painted blue-green, a perfect subtle

▼ *Floating purple dots add humor to Marcia Donahue's front stairs in Berkeley, California. Again, intensity would destroy the harmony here. The pattern brings to life these soft purples and the strong form of the potted aloe perched on the bottom stair.*

backdrop for the garden. Each fall we plant almost 3,000 tulips. Hot colors work very well—red, orange, yellow—but my favorite color scheme is crimson, white, and hot pink. With such a green garden, these complementary colors in saturated tones worked best. Pastels die a lingering death here: one year we planted soft lavender tulips. The

◄ Rockets of black-crimson glass by internationally renowned glass artist Dale Chihuly erupt from pale green male ferns. If the glass rods were fire engine red or the ferns emerald green, the contrasts would be overwhelming. Desaturating the color makes the forms of the glass and the softness of the ferns more potent.

▼ Almost a cliché of modern planting style, golden variegated and purple foliage plants like these Alternantheras *are easy to grow and eye-catching.*

▶ Silvers are bright and leaven a planting without glare, like the fuzzy silver leaves of this Plectranthus argentata *contrasting with the spiny leaves of* Acanthus montanus *'Frieling's Sensation'.*

color was too pallid and lost impact against the dark green hedges. We never repeated the mistake.

Gardening is one of the most conservative art forms, because it takes so long for a garden to be realized—plants need time to mature before the imagined becomes real. Fashion and the visual arts change rapidly; even architectural styles move faster than landscape styles. At Chatwood, Mrs. Helen Watkins had spent two decades collecting old roses and building a garden that was rich and romantic. All colors complemented the pink, mauve, cerise, and ivory of

the roses. During my second year working with her, I planted rose campion, *Lychnis coronaria*, together with a black-crimson sweet William, in one of the beds. I loved the idea of a bit of magenta livening the dusky tones of the roses and contrasting with the bloody dianthus. They grew well and bloomed the following spring as planned, and I was proud. There was just one problem. Mrs. Watkins politely let me know there was to be no magenta in her garden and could the plants please be removed, implying that sophisticated society did not appreciate such a vulgar color. Out they came.

Although "polite society" may have gardened with pastels not so long ago, in the course of the last fifteen years it has been exciting to witness a broader acceptance of color. Chartreuse and purple seem to be all the rage these days, even in the most polite company. In fact, it seems you can hardly get away from the combination in both public and private gardens. With so many golden variegated and plum foliage plants to choose from, it is easy to put striking combinations together. Colored foliage is becoming as prominent as flowering perennials and annuals. If you visit many gardens, you will see a new freedom among gardeners. As Cole Porter put it, "Anything goes."

These days, I am more interested in playing with tints (a color with white added to it) and tones (a color with black added to it) than with the whole crayon box at once. These variations of intensity provide enormous

It is a
color glutton's
paradise
out there,
so have fun

opportunity. Blacks, dark purples, deep reds—they are the bass notes that enable the light colors to shine. They are also dramatic, so they give depth to the garden. One of my favorite images to conjure is from Pepsico. The late Russell Page planted a hedge of copper beech trees to provide the backdrop for a towering Louise Nevelson sculpture, great planes of matte black steel punctured with holes and peels of metal on the surface. It sits in a star of black mondo grass on an emerald lawn. All the black consumes light, thus it must be appreciated close at hand. From a distance, the sculpture is silhouetted against the purple hedge. Only when you approach can you see the intricacies of the form.

I love black because everything else looks more vibrant with it. White has the opposite effect. We are taught that white is neutral, a color for interiors, to be painted in an eggshell finish. In the garden, however, against green and all the other colors of the rainbow, white dominates. Nothing stands out more than white, not even the most intense fire engine red. That is why it is so effec-

continues on page 105

▶ *Lamb's ears, or* **Stachys byzantina,** *is one of the standbys in the mixed border. The silver foliage can temper strong colors and liven dark tones. It is easy to grow the flower spikes, which add relief to the mounding form of most plants. The cultivar 'Big Ears' is my favorite. It is less silver, with larger leaves, and is more disease resistant.*

▲ *In the Northwest Perennial Alliance border at the Bellevue Botanical Garden in Bellevue, Washington, this simple black-and-white scheme is dramatic, demonstrating the power of white and the depth that black adds to the garden. Purple barberries,* Hydrangea macrophylla *v.* serrata *'Preziosa', and* Phalaris arundinacea *'Feesey' are all easy to grow.*

◄ *The daring colors of chartreuse and magenta are not for the faint of heart. In late May in the Northwest Perennial Alliance border, this circus of contrasting colors draws you across the lawn from the visitor center to this heroic border, where you will either scream in ecstasy or get sick to your stomach, depending on your proclivity for strong color associations. The plants are* Geranium psilostemon, Hemerocallis *cv.,* Weigela *'Briant Rubidor',* Chrysanthemum parthenium *'Aurea',* Catalpa bignonioides *'Aurea',* Rosa *cv., and* Aconitum vulparia.

Lobelia tupa, which is tender in most of the country, gives relief to the frenetically crimson-striated foliage of Canna 'Tropicana'. Again, the contrast of light and dark is as striking as chartreuse and magenta.

tive as a focal point. It draws the eye and can be seen no matter how great the distance. White is soothing, crisp, and refreshing, but it is not powerless and should not be used in the garden without thought. It can compete with the hottest pink, the most intense tangerine, the most acid yellow. I must confess I generally steer clear of white, and use it only as an accent. But when I want to make a loud, clear statement in the garden, I use it en masse. My favorite tulip planting in Silas Mountsier's garden was a drift of 350 white ones in front of an American holly hedge. The dark green holly was the perfect foil for the streak of white along the side of the garden. It was dramatic, but cold. If you want to add lightness without the glare, gray is an effective alternative—not as strong as white, but nearly as captivating.

To understand color you must be brave. Experiment, have fun, plow ahead. Accept all colors for what they can contribute. Think about the best way to achieve your intended effect. Don't exclude magenta because it is not "polite"—even a tiny bit can enliven dark and dusky pinks. It is a color glutton's paradise out there, so have fun. In the book *Artists in Their Gardens*, Seattle glass artist Ginny Ruffner explodes when asked which are her favorite colors:

"Bullshit—I never met a color I didn't like! It depends on what a plant does—they're all different, just like people, just like a piece of art. How could I choose which color I like best? It's crazy—which finger do I like best?" ■

Light

But wherever possible a tree

should be so placed that it casts its shade

across the flat lawn in the morning or evening.

The dark shadow moving across the grass,

changing in shape as the day passes,

is a magical addition to a garden view.

~

GRAHAM STUART THOMAS,

The Art of Planting

The tulip 'Orange Emperor' is set afire in the late afternoon light. It is growing here with Cornus sanguinea *'Midwinter Fire'.*

Photography has taught me a lot about seeing and appreciating the qualities of light. Midday full sun is the worst light in which to see a garden. Not that the garden looks bad—but there is no dimension. When light is hard and strong, it causes dark, deep shadows, making everything go flat. As you stroll through a garden, the light seems to have little impact because there is so much other sensory information flooding the brain. You are moving through space, so the experience is dynamic, not static. There may be smells, a breeze, staggering heat if it is summer, or a chill in late spring. You are not just seeing, you are experiencing the garden.

Light plays an important part in this experience, though, because it affects how we perceive color, defines form and space by shadow and highlight, and reinforces the obvious, such as time of day and time of year. In winter, for example, the angle of the sun on the horizon is low in the sky. In July it is high, bright, and strong. Light can be used to direct people. In a dark place, it is natural to move toward light, so arbors and alleys of trees draw us through as we pursue the light at the end of the tunnel.

My favorite light is early morning. It changes minute by minute, and the dynamic of sunrise is exhilarating. I am always rewarded when I force myself to rise early—something I don't normally like to do—to photograph a garden. One of my most memorable mornings was in June 2000 in Tom Hobbs's fantastic garden near Vancouver,

> Who can resist the delicate nature of a flower made luminous by the light passing through it?

British Columbia. I was trying to capture the sunrise over English Bay and the city skyline. I arrived just before 5 A.M. to set up the equipment on his back terrace, just as the magic started. The golden light of sunrise is exquisite. Watching the sun break over the horizon is a humbling sight, an experience many of us take for granted. The light is low, shadows are soft, and everything is bathed in gold, as if Midas has touched the world. It is hard to frame and take the pictures fast enough, because the light gets stronger second by second as the sun rises. The gentle light hardens as the sun climbs. I never feel more alive than when watching this transformation. The grogginess disappears, and adrenaline pulses. If, like me, you are not a morning person, it is worth making the effort on occasion just to experience the drama of sunrise.

Sunset, with its low golden light, is also a time when most of us enjoy our gardens. The whole process takes longer than the speeding sunrise, allowing you to absorb the quality of light at a more leisurely pace. A barbecue in summer will draw us outdoors to savor these moments with friends. Coupled with, say, a planting of Oriental lilies,

continues on page 113

▶ *There is nothing more sumptuous than the golden light of early morning. The* **Rhodochiton atrosanguineus** *is more spectacular because of the graphic, though fleeting, shadows of the birdcage and a potted agave.*

▲ *Like a more traditional Italian-inspired balustrade, this fence of vertically set pipes is functional and creates magical shadows on the walk.*

▶ *Shadows accent form in a most dramatic way. The staccato rhythm of the stone balusters is possible only when the sun is low in the sky, which is in late afternoon in this image.*

▲ *There is relief and ghostly beauty in first frost. In the wild garden at Wave Hill, New York, the crisp light of late autumn enhances the salvia's papery quality. It is always nice to look from the shadows into sunlight. The light draws you on to explore the garden and feel the remaining warmth of the October sun.*

◀ *These chairs on the lawn at Wave Hill invite you to stop and soak up what may be the last warm day in late October. The light is pale and crisp as the year moves into winter.*

which are most potently fragrant in the evening, the garden takes on a heady atmosphere.

The quality of light through the various seasons in different places is also notable. I think of light in the winter—when there is any in Seattle—as dull and wan. When I lived in New Jersey, the light in winter was thin and sharp on a sunny day, imparting no real color to the landscape it bathed. Summer light is very different: bright yellow, and very strong—bleaching and overwhelming the softer colors. Strong direct light like this dissipates pale colors, rendering them lifeless. The propensity toward saturated colors in hot, dry climates compensates for the bleaching effect of strong sunlight. In Southern California, a magenta bougainvillea seems perfectly natural, whereas in, say, a Minnesota garden, it would be shocking. That doesn't mean you shouldn't use intense colors in a temperate climate, but be aware that they are associated with heat and the tropics or the desert, so they have more impact there. I like strong colors placed where they can soak up strong light.

As I write this, I am thinking back on my own work to see if I have adhered to my own proclamations. I will plant strongly colored plants—such as impatiens—in the shade. They are durable, and their color palette is broad— I especially love the clear orange ones. On the other hand, the only places I've painted an architectural feature cobalt or canary is in sunny gardens. The quietude of a shady garden does not need the blaring intensity of such artifice. The emotional power of color can be sensed just by standing in the sun, or stepping out of it.

Winter and summer represent extremes in temperature and light intensity. Spring and autumn are more moderate. Spring seems more pronounced than fall, however, because following the dull winter days we've just endured, spring makes the world new again. During April days in Seattle, the clouds are high and dark, with great patches of blue sky showing through. The sun has not gained the intensity it will have in August, and clouds come and go, blocking out the spring sky completely or partially, making it seem ephemeral, like sunrise. Colors appear fresh and clear and pure. Pastels are at their best in this kind of light—bright, but not overpowering.

Autumn is more relaxed, like sunset. We watch the sun wane on the horizon and lose its potency to the encroaching winter. Light in early fall is rich and golden, but as Thanksgiving approaches, the light loses its warmth and flattens. Perhaps that is why we love the idea of maple trees in Vermont: they are a last great explosion of light and color. Colchicums are an autumnal favorite, the great goblet's pink-magenta provides a contrast of rich color just as so many other plants are turning pale, losing their vigor, and dying.

The broad gestures of the sun and seasons track our days and years, but smaller moments are measured by light as well. Shadows create space and rhythm in the garden. The shadows on a picket fence late in the day create a precise staccato pattern that delineates every board. The shade of a tree creates a more intimate place than the large expanse of a meadow under an open sky. The light and

dark patterns of a wisteria-covered pergola draw you through the walk. On the curved pergola Beatrix Ferrand designed in the walled garden at Old Westbury, New York (page 58), the wisteria does not smother the structure, but rather creates languorous patches of light and dark that beckon you forward.

Of course, the most charming light, which is often captured on film, is that seen through translucent flower petals. Who can resist the delicate nature of a flower made luminous by the light passing through it? Grasses are

---

▲ *This sculptural black granite fountain, designed by Topher Delaney, is made more mystical by the neon lighting.*

◀ *Light is what gives garden pools their magic, like a mirror reflecting the world back to us. Looking down to the sky gives us an unexpected pleasure. Black dyes used to suppress algae increase the reflective quality of water, as does painting the bottom of pools black or dark blue.*

The leaves of this Abyssinian banana, Ensete ventricosum 'Maurelii', act like great sails that capture the midmorning sun in this garden. The color is greatly enhanced by the backlight.

Molinia caerulea 'Skyracer' is one of my favorite grasses. It blooms for three months and is light and airy, adding volume to a planting without being visually heavy. Grasses are also spectacular because their stems are so thin they soak up the light, the way a monofilament does, breathing life into any garden scene.

nature's equivalent of fiber-optic cable. The thin stems, with flowers—subtle as they are—and later seeds, conduct light in a way that creates an incredible dynamic energy. Not only are grasses spectacular when backlit or sidelit, but they move too. They are kinetic. This quality may be why grasses have become so popular with gardeners and garden

designers. Nothing can lift a dull, heavy scene faster than adding a few grasses to the planting. At the Miller Garden, we have many dwarf conifers, which develop wonderful sculptural forms as they age (ten years or older), but they grow slowly, don't change noticeably in short time spans, and are dense, rather uninteresting lumps, especially when young. To compensate, we added a wide variety of grasses: one of my favorites is *Molinia caerulea* 'Skyracer'. This grass has green foliage that grows eighteen to twenty-four inches, but the flowering heads reach six to seven feet. They are sheer, gracefully arching, and seem to absorb light. I have seen the same variety in the Northeast, the upper Midwest, and here in the Pacific Northwest, and everywhere it performs as expected.

Light is one of the most transient characteristics in a garden composition, but with effort you can harness its ethereal qualities to create magic. ■

Form and Texture

The energy and space

around a material are as important

as the energy and space within.

~

Andy Goldsworthy,

A Collaboration with Nature

Giant Australian clams appear to clatter at you from a planting of the large Aloe striata *and the smaller* Aloe brevifolia *at Ganna Walska Lotusland, Santa Barbara, California.*

One climate in which I have yet to garden is the desert. The plants—agaves and aloes and the world of cacti and succulents—are so sculptural, so pure in form. Ganna Walska Lotusland in Santa Barbara, California, is one garden that explores this environment well. Madame Walska loved plants and went beyond just assembling collections. Everything was planted in excess and to great effect. Images pop into mind that are eerie and wonderful at the same time. Tentacles of weeping *Euphorbia insignis* at the front of the house are both animate and ominous, seemingly able to reach out and grab you if you get too close. The aloe garden includes tree aloes from Africa and the Old World—spare and gaunt, with jesterlike heads of

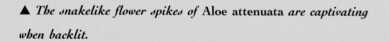

▲ *The snakelike flower spikes of* **Aloe attenuata** *are captivating when backlit.*

▶ *A jester's cap of* **Aloe spectabilis** *adds drama to any garden, whether planted in the ground or in a container in colder climates.*

foliage—and aloes used as ground covers in varied shapes, sizes, and colors. The most wonderful feature of this garden is the pool, which has a coping of abalone shells and Australian giant clam fountains. Strolling through, you cannot help but think you are strolling on the bottom of the ocean in this foreign and wonderful place.

Spiky or linear foliage plants always add excitement to the garden. The form is menacing and grabs attention quickly. Phormiums, cordylines, yuccas, and iris add dramatic form because they look so different than the rounded low silhouettes of so many plants. Add color and you add further emphasis. At the Miller Garden, for the last couple of years we have planted *Phormium* 'Color Guard' in a large stoneware container at the base of the dry hillside. It is captivating: great swords of leaves striped valentine crimson. In mid-May the *Geum* 'Red Wings' blooms, and the combination, which lasts two weeks, is a knockout. Scarlet dots hover like irradiated lightning bugs. Geums are not plants that particularly excite me, but this one, combined with the New Zealand flax, was a happy accident that we repeat every year.

Triangles and their three-dimensional counterparts, pyramids, have the same impact. Visually, they are high-energy forms, and they can even take on a mystical quality. When I was invited to plant a temporary display for the Washington Park Arboretum in Seattle, I wanted to do more than just fill up the bed with plants. I started to think about the building and the large arbor surrounding three

continues on page 127

▲ *Portable pizzazz with* Cordyline australis *'Alberti' in a container. We have eight of these cordylines and they live in different spots each summer at the Elisabeth C. Miller Botanical Garden in Seattle. The linear foliage has even more impact because each leaf is edged in cream.*

◄ Phormium *'Color Guard' is one of the best of the crimson-colored forms. The gold cone junipers echo the vertical form in the distance.*

▲ *Pyramids are full of mystical energy, and this one in Johanna Nitzke-Marquis's garden is amazing. Eighteen hundred bowling balls are both imposing and a kick in the pants.*

▶ *These inverted terra-cotta pyramids used as hanging containers are threatening but lushly beautiful. They are three feet long and nearly two feet wide, not including the hanging apparatus, and weigh almost eighty pounds empty. They were custom designed for the Washington Park Arboretum in Seattle.*

sides. I wanted to add hanging baskets, but not typical ones. Pyramids came to mind, inverted pyramids. The arbor is quite large and could hold significant weight, so we created cardboard prototypes to get the scale right, 22 inches wide and 32 inches long, then had them made of terra-cotta. They got people's attention. They looked great with the simple architecture and the arbor, while looking slightly threatening—large, pointy pots suspended in midair. We planted them with purple and golden foliage plants, with a shock of crayon orange impatiens.

Circles have the same potent dynamic effect in the landscape, because balls connote kinetic energy. Alliums always remind me of playing T-ball as a child (the game in which the ball is batted off a rubber post). I can't help but think of the game when I see these bulbs in flower— I'd love to bat the purple heads off into oblivion.

Form imposed in a garden layout as a whole can be equally exciting. I have always admired the collaboration of Gertrude Jekyll and Edwin Lutyens. Lutyens was an English architect and garden designer working in the late nineteenth and early twentieth centuries. He used pure and simple geometries, which I find refreshing and appealing to my own tastes. I much prefer highly organized and geometric gardens over wavy, wiggly lines, which can be too indiscriminate. Strong forms organize and provide focus in a garden. Landscape architect Steve Martino, has designed gardens with crisp bold architectural lines in simple forms, often—but by no means exclusively—in colored adobe. I think gardens should be lucid if nothing

▲ *Tom Hobbs creates shocking beauty with this arrangement of exquisitely crafted Italian terra-cotta planted with a selection of echeverias. The repetition of the circular forms is soothing.*

◀ *This spiral of wrought iron is mesmerizing alone, and is even more amazing with the dying flower heads of alliums 'Purple Sensation'.*

▲ *An explosion of silver cardoon,* Cynara cardunculus, *is a bold statement wherever you plant it. This artichoke relative has giant stalks, to eight feet, of thistle flowers in midsummer, but I would be happier if it never flowered.*

▶ *This exclamation mark of* Taxus baccata *'Bean Pole' is even more striking emerging from the black* Ophiopogon. *The* Agave americana *'Mediopicta' is my favorite for containers. The cream-striped blue leaves are wonderful. It is difficult to find, and I buy specimens whenever I get the chance because they are rarely available. It is easy to grow and long-lived, and clients love its menacing beauty.*

else, and strong geometry linked to the architecture is one clear way of achieving this.

A display garden for a wholesale nursery that Steve designed changed the way I think about gardens. One of my favorite parts is a low serpentine wall clad in green glass tiles that intersects a circular seating area made of concrete blocks (page 50). Juxtaposed against the block construction, a crude material, the clean geometry of the circle stands out. The playfulness of the wriggling wall intersecting the space is beautiful—like a primordial sperm fertilizing an egg.

Simple geometries like this, one imposed upon the other, are very striking for the tension they create. I used the trick in Silas Mountsier's garden. I designed a round pool with a square terrace imposed over the circular form (page 86). The terrace is also raised six inches above the existing garden, so that you have to step up onto it, and the water level is lowered to a foot below the terrace. The square terrace dominates the pool, and the slight change in grade accentuates the feeling. It feels secure to sit on one of the two benches and watch the golden ornamental trout swim back and forth around the pool. A variety of grasses and bamboos around the pool encloses the space and makes a little haven in the larger garden. It is my favorite spot.

Like color, texture works best when thought out in relative terms. Most plants are a medium to medium-fine texture, creating a quiet background in the same way that green does. Once we begin to introduce extremes, we can

understand what a medium-textured plant is. In a temperate climate, few plants have excessively large foliage; when we see large leaves they are usually on bog or marginal plants with high water needs, such as *Rodgersia*, *Ligularia*, and the king of all (but only adapted to the Pacific Northwest), *Gunnera*, with five-foot-diameter leaves. The tropics and subtropics are a different world altogether. Large, bold foliage plants are plentiful, thus we associate large foliage with warm climates. In recent years, bananas and cannas have been all the rage—large, colorful leaves appear even more dramatic in regions where they do not grow naturally. We are not used to seeing these plants and, for some, seeing them in New York, Wisconsin, Kansas, or Oregon gardens is disquieting. The Victorians were fond of these tropical oddities and used them in their gardens with great flair and abandon. What's old is new again!

Large leaves contrast dramatically with surrounding vegetation and stand out or can provide strong seasonal focal points. Elephant ears, *Colocasia esculenta*, are common and cheap and, combined with grasses, are even more dazzling. Grasses add movement, and the fineness of their leaves contrasts with nearly everything else. They are adaptable, and you can find one to suit any environment

▶ *Grasses add life and movement to any garden. This old standby, maiden grass, or* **Miscanthus sinensis 'Gracillimus'**, *was a favorite with Victorian gardeners. It is at its best in late summer, when the feather-duster flower heads emerge—and like all grasses it is heavenly when backlit.*

◀ *In the monocot border at Wave Hill, the simplicity of this combination is no less dramatic for the contrast in scale and texture of the elephant ear with the fountain grass. Broad contrast always increases the tension, and thus the impact, in whatever you are doing.*

▶ *The withered leaves of this tree aloe are so textural you want to reach out and experience them firsthand; the pattern of strong light and deep shadow enhances it.*

---

in any size. One of my favorite plantings with grasses is the monocot border at Wave Hill in New York. Marco Polo Stufano, head gardener there for nearly forty years, has used a variety of commonly available grasses mixed with asparagus, and for a little punch has thrown in cannas, elephant ears, potted date palms, and potted cordylines. Even with a limited range of colors, the planting is dynamic, with strong contrasts in texture. ∎

Features and Accents

Statues have been used

in many different ways,

but the underlying reason for their use

has been the same.

They are the great humanizers,

by which man projects his personality

and love of creation

into the realm of nature.

~

SYLVIA CROWE,

Garden Design

Large pots of lavender pink Colchicums on the stairs and landing at the Miller Botanical Garden in September are ephemeral, lasting only a couple of weeks. Containers are mobile, so as they fade, the flowers are carted away and planted in the garden.

▶ *This Beaux Arts fountain in a private garden in Santa Barbara, California, has an elegant stature and presence. The simplicity of the composition and the bold form give the scene impact.*

Water adds dimension to any garden, and it can be used in a variety of ways. It can be an extravagant element, such as the water parterres at the Villa Lante, one of the many great Italian gardens built in the sixteenth and seventeenth centuries. It can be monumental and boisterous, exemplifying great force, such as the Four Corners fountain in Portland, Oregon, designed by Lawrence Halprin, who wants us to experience the rush and force of a mountain stream. It can be still, quiet, and reflect its surroundings and the sky overhead. It can be very small, sweet, and as simple as a birdbath.

Using water as a primary feature takes careful planning and engineering. Generally, garden designers keep water features small and manageable. Designers in the Beaux Arts tradition of the early twentieth century drew their inspiration from the Italians, using highly formal garden pools as the focal point of a space. Modern gardens can use countless materials with more eccentric approaches. Artists David Little and George Lewis from Bainbridge Island, Washington, add color and a sense of playfulness to classically inspired columns, plumbing them to make slowly dripping columns that lull you into a peaceful trance. They take full advantage of the lyrical sounds of dripping water in their works.

Still pools used for reflecting are best achieved when the pool bottom is painted dark or the water is dyed black. The dark color makes clearer reflections. I like the black dye and the mystery it gives to a reflecting pond. It also reduces light penetration in the water, thus reducing algae growth. Water does require engineering, and you will be surprised at the effort required to keep it fresh and sparkling. Aquatic systems need constant monitoring and fine-tuning, but they are worth the effort for the quietude they impart. Even in the smallest garden, used in the simplest ways,

▲ *Snuffling in European ginger and painted fern, this lead pig looks right at home and is a pleasant surprise just off the main terrace in Silas Mountsier's New Jersey garden.*

◀ *The artists David Little and George Lewis are enamored of water and its many possibilities. They have made a basin that is functional and uniquely sculptural here. It is planted with one of my favorite miniature water lilies, 'Helvola'.*

water adds a sense of depth and dimension unrivaled by any other single garden element.

Sculpture can express the spirit of a garden—or garden maker—in a succinct way. Like a poem, a sculpture is a distillation of ideas and emotions, a visual statement that cuts to the quick with sparseness and accuracy. It can be classical or contemporary, abstract or figurative. Whatever the form, it should be used thoughtfully. Large commanding pieces need careful placement and can be used as focal points in primary views. Smaller, less significant pieces can be used as asides in less prominent locations. Most important, to be used to maximum effect, sculpture needs air—space and a setting that allow it to be showcased. Too many sculptures or too large a sculpture in a small space can make the garden look cluttered.

Like water, sculpture can consume a garden. A very large piece may require a concrete base. Pedestals and plinths are not as common in the garden as they are indoors, but they are an effective way to highlight important smaller pieces. A pedestal can be temporary and mobile, from a simple wooden box to a permanent plinth of cut limestone or poured concrete. I prefer modern, abstract sculpture, but all art pieces in the garden should have a strong, clear outline that reads well and is visually clearly defined. Complex shapes are best set against simple backdrops so they can be clearly seen and understood. If your garden is planted in a complex way, simple forms will complement rather than compete with the vegetation.

Pots are the most common objects in a garden. Whether empty or planted, the choice of container should resonate with the garden's style and meet functional needs. If you plan to leave your containers in the garden year-round, choose the material accordingly. Terra-cotta does not tolerate harsh winter climates: stone, cast concrete, cast iron, and fiberglass are sturdier. Large containers have more visual impact and are easier to care for because they can hold more soil for root space and water retention. I have definite preferences when it comes to containers. I like groups of simply planted pots rather than lots of pots with many kinds of plants. This makes for a stronger, more dramatic and direct impact. Pots can be easily rearranged to create new compositions. Large pots with complex plantings are best in simple settings, where the variety can be appreciated and does not distract from plantings in the garden itself. Personal taste rules here—if you like lots of stuff and have a dense aesthetic, you can create amazing puzzlelike effects. Careful arrangement is important, so that all the parts harmonize and do not overwhelm. I fall somewhere in the middle. I am not a minimalist, but I also dislike gardens that are so visually dense they appear chaotic.

Furniture is an essential element in any garden if you plan to live in it rather than just look at it. Two essential points: furniture should be visually sympathetic in style, like containers, and it should be comfortable. There is more selection for those who prefer traditional styles, but

continues on page 144

▲ *Peering through tropical foliage, a granite baboon is a strong focal point at the end of the lawn in Silas Mountsier's garden.*

▶ *Sculpture, like no other element, brings a strong sense of creativity and humanity to any garden. Isamu Noguchi is one of the most inspired of twentieth-century sculptors. His work is beautifully presented at the Isamu Noguchi Garden Museum in Long Island City, New York.*

▲ *The luxury of plants in pots is their mobility and changeability. Purple fountain grass and various colored forms of* Alternanthera *are the central focus of the flower garden at Wave Hill in the Bronx, New York.*

▶ *Innovation and experimentation are always fun. This tepee of* Thunbergia gregorii *looks great with* Manihot esculenta *'Variegata', or the variegated tapioca plant, and* Coleus *'Japanese Brocade', also at Wave Hill.*

modern styles are fast becoming more available. Good garden furniture is expensive, so you will not likely be changing it often. Readily available plastic is cheap but contributes little other than meeting the most basic functional needs. Discount stores now offer wider varieties and better-looking furniture if you are willing to take time

▼ *This lush arrangement of pots and tender plants greets visitors to offices at the Scott Arboretum at Swarthmore College, just south of Philadelphia. Containers are a cheap way to practice zonal denial.*

▲ In these playful renditions of the Rietveld chair, an icon of modernist design from 1918, Bob Dash has painted them sunshine yellow with lavender arms in his garden, Madoo, on eastern Long Island, New York. I can think of nothing more pleasant than to be sitting with him, sipping martinis, and wasting away a summer afternoon.

to search. Teak now comes in a variety of styles, from classic to updated. It looks great in the garden and acquires a beautiful patina as it ages. It is also durable. Wicker needs protection and annual maintenance if it is going to endure. I am most excited about the variety of metals now available, from galvanized metal to aluminum and stainless

◀ A traditional-style chaise lounge invites you to dream of languorous afternoons with a good book in the private paradise of Tom Hobbs and Brent Beattie. The chair's style fits perfectly with the stucco wall and tiled terrace. Continuity of style is essential if the garden is to be cohesive.

steel. These materials are long lasting and impart a sophisticated, urbane look to the garden.

No matter what features you add to your garden, the most important factor is that each item be simpatico with the setting. Drastic digressions in character can make an individual piece seem out of place and can destroy the mood. That doesn't mean you should eschew eclecticism: just make sure that sculpture, containers, and furniture work in concert with your garden, not against it. ■

Don't Just Stand There—
Say Something!

The size of a garden has very little to do with its merit. It is merely an accident relating to the circumstances of the owner. It is the size of his heart and brain and goodwill that make his garden either delightful or dull, as the case may be, and either leave it at the monotonous dead level, or raise it, in whatever degree he may, towards that of a work of art.

~

GERTRUDE JEKYLL,

Wood and Garden

The Davis garden in El Paso, Texas, is bold in spirit and does not shy from controversy. It is a mazelike arrangement of rooms, each painted a different color inside and out, each a minimal composition that will leave you smiling, grimacing, or scratching your head.

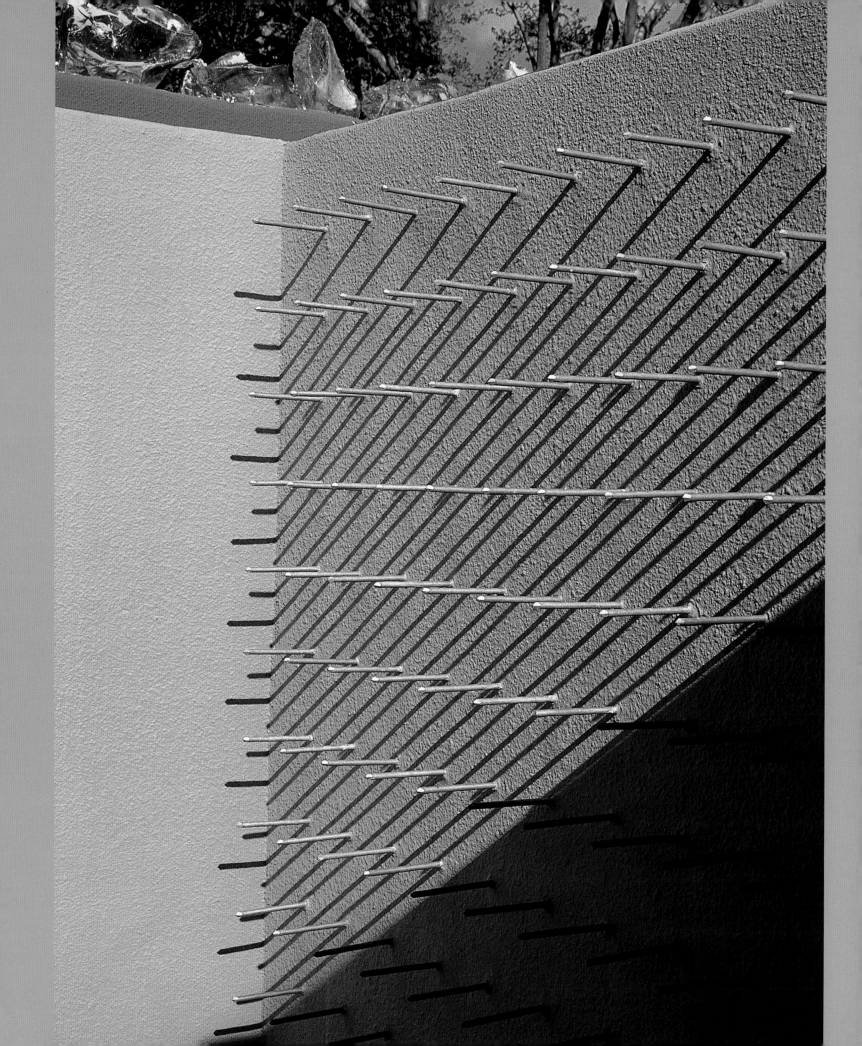

◄ Brutally striking, these nails, set in a lipstick pink stucco wall, scare most visitors. The changing shadows animate the room and keep you coming back.

▼ Across the way from the room of nails, this pipe organ cactus arrangement is less threatening, but still makes you pay attention.

Many of us forget that we are saying something about ourselves when we embark on this journey called gardening. The best gardens are those made by someone who has wrestled his or her statement to the ground and tried to say something beyond "Aren't these beautiful plants, and lovely paving, and a well-crafted fence?" Style can converge with theme to reflect the heart and soul of the owner to such a degree that after we have visited a garden we know that person better.

Style should strongly reflect the architecture of the home. To diverge drastically from such dominant cues spells disaster—discord will be the result if you ignore this basic tenet. Three gardens come to mind that are very different, but whose underlying style and ideas come screaming through. First I am thinking of Heronswood, on the Kitsap Peninsula in western Washington State, the home of Dan Hinkley and Robert Jones and their now internationally renowned nursery. Their modest home sits demurely in the midst of a garden that is all about the beauty and wonder of plants, executed with an enthusiasm

▲ *Brian Coleman's and Howard Cohen's home on Queen Anne Hill in Seattle is overwhelming because there is so much visual input competing for attention. The tall Victorian house and its garden are not visually restful, but are fun to absorb. The combination is an education in a forgotten style of architecture and garden design.*

that is unrivaled. The home sits near the back half of a three-acre garden, nearly disappearing among the extravagantly beautiful vegetation. Where there are no direct connections to terraces or entrances to the home, the space is obliterated by vine-covered trellises or small trees.

Brian Coleman's and Howard Cohen's garden on Queen Anne Hill in Seattle is similar, but distinctive in its own right. They have rebuilt their house to reflect Victorian tastes that I doubt the Victorians could have executed so supremely. This modest home is on a lot that is a typical size for its neighborhood, probably less than a quarter of an acre. What it lacks in size, it more than makes up for in impact. The house and garden are inextricable, both dense with details that are hallmarks of the Victorian age. It is dizzying to see the front garden against the backdrop of the home's opulent architecture. Griffins flanking the front stairs and a lamp-blacked, gold-trimmed iron fountain are hallmarks of the period. The plantings are saturated with color, complementing the house's rich color scheme and high contrasts of form and texture. The house and garden are a fantasy that leaps from the style pages of the late nineteenth century.

Last is a garden in El Paso, Texas, owned by Ann and Sam Davis and designed by Boston landscape architect Martha Schwartz. The hot, dry climate of southwest Texas was the perfect place to use stucco, inspired by the late Mexican architect Luis Barragan, whose spare modernist style has become familiar in modern architecture and landscape architecture in the desert Southwest. Ann loves modern design that is clean and spare but distinctive, with loads of personality. She wanted a garden that would

Plants reign supreme here. They are arranged in a naturalistic style that harkens back to Gertrude Jekyll in the English cottage style, which Dan does with drama and a flair that would make even Gertrude green with envy. Color and texture and sheer variety abound in a rich, almost baroque, manner. The garden spaces are simply laid out, in a way that does not compete with the plantings but complements the beautiful combinations. The garden is a tour de force that grows to the point of being overwhelming in its staggering complexity. It is the ultimate plant lover's paradise, as beautiful as the plants are varied.

reflect this desire, that would make a statement. The Davises' garden does. There is no doubt that it is in the Southwest, with its architectural references, and the few plants are all cacti. The garden is a series of cubes, each painted a different color inside and out, and each with a different focus. Small windows are cut to form sight lines

---

▲ *'Paul's Himalayan' musk rose drapes over the vine arbor in the garden behind Dan Hinkley's and Robert Jones's home at Heronswood. No plant collector worth his salt has not heard of this internationally famous nursery and garden. Dan's rich style of planting is staggeringly beautiful, and his nursery is the mecca of gardeners in search of new and unusual plants.*

◄ *Deutzia 'Magicien' is fecund with bloom in the perennial border. Dan Hinkley's gardening style has English roots, but he adds an up-to-date flair that is distinctly American.*

down passages and through the walls that define the rooms. You cannot help but be drawn to these Alice-in-Wonderland-like views. The windows are not at eye level, so you find yourself bending or crouching slightly to get the perfect look. They are fun, whimsical. They draw you into the maze.

My favorite room is painted pink on the interior, with one wall set with a grid of large nails: it is horrifying and wondrous. The light patterns are captivating, and you find yourself returning to this garden room just to see how the shadows have changed. Each room is equally spare, some more unsettling than others. It is not a garden of pretty things, but more like the house of wonders at an amusement park—beautiful in an eerie way that leaves you wondering what the maker intended. I think Ann wanted to be a provocateur, because the effect is shocking. If this was not her intent, it is certainly what she achieved. I find the garden hauntingly beautiful and think back on my visit often. Such a garden is daring and playful, perfect in its hot, dry climate. The intensity of the colored walls defies the relentless sun of El Paso in August.

Each of these three gardens represents a clear vision that is bold and thoughtful, that demonstrates passion and an indomitable pursuit of that vision. I admire these owners' willingness to say something about who they are in making gardens that reflect their values. Gardening is about being clear-minded in your goals and having a dogged determination to realize them. These are the kinds of gardens I want to see, experience, and learn from. ■

Gardens You Shouldn't Miss Seeing

These are the public gardens pictured in the book or those that I feel are of exceptional merit. It is by no means a complete list.

■ California

Marcia Donahue
3017 Wheeler Street
Berkeley, CA 94705
E-mail: Thanks2flora@earthlink.net
(Open on Sunday afternoons only)

Ganna Walska Lotusland
Tel.: 805.969.3767
Fax: 805.969.4423
Web: lotusland.org
(Open by appointment only)

J. Paul Getty Museum
17985 Pacific Coast Highway
Malibu, CA 90265
Tel.: 310.459.7611
Fax: 310.454.6633
Web: getty.edu

Ruth Bancroft Garden
PO Box 30845
Walnut Creek, CA 94598
Tel.: 925.210.9663
Web: ruthbancroftgarden.org
(Open by appointment only)

■ New Jersey

Willowwood Arboretum
PO Box 1295
Morristown, NJ 07962
Tel.: 201.326.7600
Fax: 201.644.2726

■ New York

Brooklyn Botanic Garden
1000 Washington Avenue
Brooklyn, NY 11225
Tel.: 718.623.7200
Web: bbg.org

Central Park Conservatory Garden
Fifth Avenue and 105th Street
New York, NY

Isamu Noguchi Garden Museum
32-37 Vernon Boulevard
Long Island City, NY 11106
Tel.: 718.204.7088
Web: noguchi.org

LongHouse Reserve
133 Hands Creek Road
East Hampton, NY 11937
Tel.: 631.329.3568
Web: longhouse.org

Madoo
Box 362
Sagaponack, NY 11962
Tel.: 516.537.0802
Web: madoo.org

Old Westbury Gardens
71 Old Westbury Road
Old Westbury, NY 11569
Tel.: 516.333.0048
Web: oldwestburygardens.org

Kandall Sculpture Garden
PepsiCo Headquarters
700 Anderson Hill Road
Purchase, NY 10577
Tel.: 914.253.2900

Wave Hill
675 W. 252nd Street
Bronx, NY 10471
Tel.: 718.549.2055
Fax: 718.884.8952
Web: wavehill.org

■ Pennsylvania

Chanticleer
786 Church Road
Wayne, PA 19087
Tel.: 610.687.4163
Web: chanticleergarden.org

Scott Arboretum
500 College Avenue
Swarthmore, PA 19081
Tel.: 610.328.8025
Web: scottarboretum.org

■ Texas

Peckerwood Garden
20571 FM 359
Hempstead, TX 77445
Tel.: 979.826.3232
Fax: 979.826.0522
Web: peckerwoodgarden.com
(Open by appointment only)

■ Washington

Bellevue Botanical Garden
PO Box 40536
Bellevue, WA 98015
Tel.: 425.451.3755
Web: bellevuebotanical.org

Bloedel Reserve
7571 NE Dolphin Drive
Bainbridge Island, WA 98110
Tel.: 206.842.7631
Fax: 206.842.8970
Web: bloedelreserve.org
(Open by appointment only)

E. B. Dunn Garden
PO Box 77126
Seattle, WA 98177
Tel.: 206.362.0933
Web: dunngarden.org

Elisabeth C. Miller Botanical Garden
PO Box 77377
Seattle, WA 98177
Tel.: 206.362.8612 ➤

Fax: 206.362.4136
Web: millergarden.org
(Open by appointment only)

Heronswood
7530 288th Street NE
Kingston, WA 98346
Tel.: 360.297.4172
Fax: 360.297.8321
Web: heronswoodwood.com

Little and Lewis Studios
1940 Wingpoint Way
Bainbridge Island, WA 98110
Tel.: 206.842.8327
Web: littleandlewis.com
(Open by appointment only)

Washington Park Arboretum
University of Washington
Box 358010
Seattle, WA 98195
Tel.: 206.543.8800
Web: dept.washington.edu.wpa

■ England

Sissinghurst
Near Cranbrook
Kent TN17 2AB
Tel.: 44.1580.712850
Fax: 44.1580.713911

Great Dixter
Northium, Rye
East Sussex TN31 6PH
Tel.: 44.1797.252878

■ Netherlands

Piet and Anja Oudolf's Nursery
Broekstr 17
6999DE Hummelo
The Netherlands
Tel.: 31.314.381120

A Few Nurseries

Here are a few mail-order nurseries that are invaluable sources for me.

Ashwood
Greenforge, Kingswinford
West Midlands DY6 0AE
England
Tel.: 44.1384.401996
Fax: 44.1384.40110
Web: ashwood-nurseries.co.uk
Seeds of hellebores by color and assorted other collector's genera

Kurt Bluemel, Inc.
2740 Greene Lane
Baldwin, MD 21013-9523
Tel.: 800.248.7584
Grasses, bamboos and other perennials

Brent and Becky's Bulbs
7463 Heath Trail
Gloucester, VA 23061
Tel.: 877.661.2852
Web: brentandbeckysbulbs.com
A wide assortment of bulbs

Caladium World
PO Box 629
Sebring, FL 33871-0629
Tel.: 863.385.7661
Web: caladium.com
Caladium tubers in bulk

Camellia Forest Nursery
125 Carolina Forest Road
Chapel Hill, NC 27516
Trees and shrubs

Canyon Creek Nursery
3527 Dry Creek Road
Oroville, CA 95965
Tel.: 530.533.2166
Web: canyoncreeknursery.com
Limited list of very choice perennials

Chiltern Seeds
Bortree Stile, Ulverston
Cumbria LA12 7PB
England
Tel.: 44.1229.581137
An expansive list of perennial and annual seeds

Fairweather Gardens
PO Box 330
Greenwich, NJ 08323
Tel.: 856.451.6261
Web: fairweathergardens.com
Choice list of woody plants in larger sizes

Forest Farm
990 Tetherhow Road
Williams, OR 97544
Tel.: 541.846.7269
Web: forestfarm.com
An infinite list of woody plants

Glasshouse Works
PO Box 97
Stewart, OH 45778
Tel.: 740.662.2142
Web: glasshouseworks.com
Great list of tender plants

Going Bananas
24401 SW 197th Avenue
Homestead, FL 33031-1174
Tel.: 305.247.0397
Web: going-bananas.com
Bananas

Gossler Farms
1200 Weaver Road
Springfield, OR 97478-9691
Magnolias and other hard-to-find trees and shrubs

Heronswood
7530 288th Street NE
Kingston, WA 98346
Tel.: 360.297.4172
Fax: 360.297.8321
Web: heronswoodwood.com
A tour de force list of everything rare and choice

Logee's Greenhouses
141 North Street
Danielson, CT 06239
Tel.: 888.330.8038
Web: logees.com
Wide range of tropicals

Odyssey Bulbs
8984 Meadow Lane
Berrien Springs, MI 49103
Tel.: 616.471.4642
Web: odysseybulbs.com
Rare and hard-to-find bulbs

Plant Delights Nursery
9241 Sauls Road
Raleigh, NC 27603
Tel.: 919.772.4794
Web: plantdel.com
Great selections of perennials and odd plants

Reath Nursery
County Road 577, N-195
Vulcan, MI 49892
Tel.: 906.563.9777
Tree and herbaceous peonies

Stokes Tropicals
PO Box 9868
New Iberia, LA 70562
Tel.: 800.624.9706

Web: stokestropicals.com
Cool plants for the Southern garden and tender for the rest of us

Thompson and Morgan Seed Co.
PO Box 1308
Jackson, NJ 08527
Tel.: 800.274.7333
Web: thompson-morgan.com
Expansive list of seeds

Van Engelen Inc.
23 Tulip Drive
Bantam, CT 06750
Tel.: 860.567.8734
Web: vanengelen.com
Great selection of bulbs for quantity uses

Vintage Gardens
2833 Old Gravenstein Highway S.
Sebastopol, CA 95472
Tel.: 707.829.2035
Web: vintagegardens.com
A staggering selection of old roses

Woodlanders
1128 Colleton Avenue
Aiken, GA 29801
Tel.: 803648.7522
Web: woodlanders.net
Cool woody plants

Yucca Do Nursery
PO Box 907
Hempstead, TX 77445
Tel.: 979.826.4550
Web: yuccado.com
Varied selection of perennials and woody plants— mostly for warmer climates

A Few of My Favorite Designers

This is by no means a comprehensive list of designers nationwide. These are a very few of the garden designers/landscape architects whose work I have experienced firsthand and admire. All work nationally and some internationally. If you have enjoyed what you have seen of my work in this book, I can supply a full range of garden-design services. I can be reached at:

Richard Hartlage, PO Box 77377, Seattle, WA 98177; Tel. 206-860-0337; e-mail: richardh@millergarden.org

Butterfly Ridge Design and Works
PO Box 158
Carboro, NC 27510
Tel.: 919.933.1933
Fax: 919.933.1988

Topher Delaney Inc.
156 S. Park
San Francisco, CA 94107 ➤

Tel.: 415.896.2998
Fax: 415.896.2995

Steve Martino Associates
3336 N. 32nd Street
Phoenix, AZ 85018
Tel.: 602.957.6150

Oehme, van Sweden & Associates Inc.
800 G Street SE
Washington, DC 2003-2816
Tel.: 202.546.7575
Fax: 202.546.1035

Martha Schwartz, Inc.
147 Sherman Street, Suite 200
Cambridge, MA 02140 ➤

Tel.: 617.661.8141
Fax: 617.661.8707
Web: marthaschwartz.com

Withey-Price Landscape Design
PO Box 77321
Seattle, WA 98177
Tel.: 206.364.2225

Photographic, Garden & Designer Credits

All photographs are by author except where noted.

1 E.B. Dunn Garden, Seattle, WA; designer, Withey-Price Landscape Design

2 Ann and Sam Davis Garden, El Paso, TX; designer, Martha Schwartz Inc.

6 Ganna Walska Lotusland, Santa Barbara, CA

8 Valerie Easton garden, Seattle, WA

10 Elisabeth C. Miller Botanical Garden, Seattle, WA

12 Davis garden

13 Graeme Hardie garden, Nutley, NJ; designer, Richard W. Hartlage

14 Arid Zone Trees, Phoenix, AZ; designer, Steve Martino and Associates

17 Ganna Walska Lotusland

18 Easton garden, Seattle, WA

20 Thomas Hobbs and Brent Beattie garden, Vancouver, BC

22–25 Wave Hill, Bronx, NY

26 Easton garden

27 Stateler/Giddens garden, Phoenix, AZ; designer, Steve Martino and Associates

29 Chatwood, Hillsborough, NC

30, 31 Willowwood Arboretum, Chester, NC

32 Frederick garden, Wilmington, DE.

34 Hardie garden

36–39 Both photographs by Harpur Garden Library. Leichtag Family Healing Garden at Children's Hospital and Health Center in San Diego, CA; designer, Topher Delaney Inc.

40 Heronswood, Kingston, WA

43 Piet and Anja Oudolf garden, Hummelo, Netherlands

45 Arid Zone Trees, Phoenix, AZ

46, 47 Hardie garden

48–50 Arid Zone Trees

51 Larry and Susan Winn garden, Seattle, WA; designer Richard W. Hartlage

52, 53 Ganna Walska Lotusland

54 Photograph by Harpur Garden Library Leichtag Family Healing Garden at Children's Hospital and Health Center in San Diego, CA; designer, Topher Delaney Inc.

55 Ganna Walska Lotusland

56–57 Little and Lewis, Bainbridge Island, WA

58–59 Old Westbury Gardens, Old Westbury, NY; designer, Beatrix Ferrand

60 Stateler/Giddens garden

62–68 Hardie garden

70–73 Sissinghurst Castle and gardens, Kent, England

74 Silas Mountsier garden, Nutley, NJ; designer, Richard W. Hartlage

75 Hardie garden

76 Kandall Sculpture Garden, Purchase, NY; designer, Russell Page

77 Davis garden

79 Stateler/Giddens garden

80–83 Northwest Perennial Alliance border at Bellevue Botanical Garden; designers, Carey Becker, Bob Lilly, Charles Price, and Glenn Withey

84, 85 Easton garden

86, 87 Mountsier garden

88 Great Dixter, East Sussex, England

90, 91 Brian Coleman and Howard Cohen, Seattle, WA; designer, Withey-Price Landscape Design

92 E.B. Dunn Garden

92 Oudolf garden

96 Wells-Medina Nursery, Medina, WA; designer, Withey-Price Landscape Design

95 Easton garden

96 Arid Zone Trees

97 Marcia Donahue and Mark Bullwinkle garden, Berkeley, CA

98 Photo by Dan Hinkley, LongHouse Reserve, East Hampton, NY; glass art by Dale Chihuly

99 left and right: Wave Hill

101 Easton garden

102, 103 Northwest Perennial Alliance Border

104 Hobbs/Beattie garden

106 Elisabeth C. Miller Botanical Garden

109 Hobbs/Beattie garden

110 Photo by Harpur Garden Library, Che garden, San Francisco, CA; designer Topher Delaney Inc.

111-114 Wave Hill

115 Photo by Harpur Garden Library, designer Topher Delaney Inc.

116 Hardie garden

117 Elisabeth C. Miller Botanical Garden

118–121 Ganna Walska Lotusland

122, 123 Elisabeth C. Miller Botanical Garden

124 Photo by Johanna Nitzke Marquis. Johanna Nitzke and Dick Marquis garden

125 Washington Park Arboretum, Seattle, WA; pots designed and planted by Richard W. Hartlage

126, 127 Hobbs/Beattie garden

129 Linda Cochran garden, Bainbridge Island, WA

127 Heronswood

125 Easton garden

132 Wave Hill

133 Ganna Walska Lotusland

134 Elisabeth C. Miller Botanical Garden

137 Private garden, Santa Barbara, CA; designer, Lockwood DeForest

138 Little and Lewis garden

139, 140 Mountsier garden

141 Isamu Noguchi Garden Museum, Long Island City, NY

142, 143 Wave Hill

144 Scott Arboretum, Swarthmore, PA

145 Madoo, Sagaponack, NY

146 Hobbs/Beattie garden

148, 151 Davis garden

152, 153 Coleman garden

154, 155 Heronswood

Suggested Reading List

Bradley-Hole, Christopher. *The Minimalist Garden.* London: Mitchell Beazley, 1999.

Brooks, John. *Natural Landscapes.* New York: DK Publishing, 1998.

Church, Thomas. *Gardens are for People.* New York: Reinhold Publishing, 1955.

Conran, Terence, and Dan Pearson. *The Essential Garden Book.* New York: Crown, 1998.

Cooper, Guy, and Gordon Taylor. *Gardens for the Future.* New York: The Monacelli Press, 2000.

Cooper, Guy, and Gordon Taylor. *Paradise Transformed.* New York: The Monacelli Press, 1996.

Dickey, Page. *Breaking Ground: Portraits of Ten Garden Designers.* New York: Artisan, 1997.

Eliovson, Sima. *The Gardens of Roberto Burle Marx.* Portland, OR: Sagapress/Timber Press, 1991.

Hobbs, Thomas. *Shocking Beauty.* Boston: Periplus, 1999.

Jekyll, Gertrude. *Colour Schemes for the Flower Garden.* Salem, NH: The Ayer Company, 1983.

Oehme, Wolfgang, James Van Sweden, and Susan Rademacher. *Bold Romantic Gardens.* Washington, D.C.: Spacemaker Press, 1998.

Oudolf, Piet. *Designing with Plants.* Portland, OR: Timber Press, 1999.

Page, Russell. *The Education of a Gardener.* London: Collins, 1983.

Shepherd, J.C., and Geoffrey Jellicoe. *Italian Gardens of the Renaissance.* New York: Princeton Architectural Press, 1993.

Thomas, Graham Stuart. *The Art of Planting.* London: J. M. Dent, 1984.

Index